A Friend in the Business

Honest Advice for Anyone
Trying to Break In to
Television Writing

Robert Masello

A Perigee Book

A Perigee Book
Published by The Berkley Publishing Group
A division of Penguin Putnam Inc.
375 Hudson Street
New York, New York 10014

First edition: May 2000

Published simultaneously in Canada.

The Penguin Putnam Inc. World Wide Web site address is
http://www.penguinputnam.com

Library of Congress Cataloging-in-Publication Data

Masello, Robert.
    A friend in the business : honest advice for anyone trying to break in to television writing / Robert Masello.—1st ed.
        p. cm.
    ISBN 0-399-52602-1
    1. Television authorship. 2. Television authorship—Vocational guidance. I. Title.

PN1992.7 .M29 2000
808.2'25—dc21

                                                                99-058604

Printed in the United States of America

10 9 8 7 6 5 4 3 2 1

For Laurie, my own best friend,
who keeps the dog groomed, the roses in bloom,
and our little household humming

No man but a blockhead ever wrote except for money.

—Dr. Johnson

Contents

Reading Advisory   xiii

Part I: Slouching Toward Hollywood

OUR HERO ARRIVES   3
In Los Angeles, only a chump writes books

HUBRIS   7
If you think TV looks easy, look again

STORMING THE BARRICADES   10
The TV fortress may be strong, but it's not impregnable

A FRIEND IN THE BUSINESS   16
Why won't anybody extend a helping hand?

SO, WHAT DOES IT TAKE TO BE A TV WRITER?   20
There must be some reason they make so much money

"AND THEN WHAT HAPPENS?"   23
Without a story to tell, you don't have a script

DECISIONS, DECISIONS   26
You can laugh, or you can cry, but you can't do both

Contents

Part II: Spec Fever

ON SPEC   33
A spec script is like the army—it's not just a job, it's an adventure

MEET THE CANDIDATES   38
Only certain shows are spec-worthy—how do you pick 'em?

GREAT EX-SPEC-TATIONS   46
Hope is the thing your friends are out to kill

PAPERING THE TOWN   50
Trust everyone . . . trust no one

Part III: Agents of Influence

SECRET AGENT MAN   57
Getting an agent shouldn't be this hard

"YOU THINK *YOUR* AGENT IS BAD?"   60
Big agencies, smaller boutiques—lousy service is available anywhere you go

BOOSTER SHOTS   66
If your agent isn't your cheerleader, who will be?

THE DOTTED LINE   69
Once you sign with an agency, how long will it be before you get your soul back?

TROUBLED TIMES   74
When Mr. Trouble comes around, let your agent answer the door

Part IV: Pitching to Win

PERFECT PITCH   79
Never take the mound until you've warmed up

INSIDE INFORMATION   84
What do you know that they don't?

THE WINDUP   86
You're only as funny as your sweatshirt

THE PITCH   90
Remember, this is one pitch you want *them to connect with*

THE UNCERTAINTY PRINCIPLE   97
Assume victory until otherwise informed

CALL-BACKS   99
Nimble fingers are needed to tie up those loose ends

Part V: Script for Success

A SIMPLE PLAN   109
Writing without an outline is like trekking without a compass

GO TO SCRIPT!   113
The starting pistol has fired—now run!

TAKING NOTES   118
If your skin isn't thick, wear corduroy

Part VI: Career Moves

LAWS, SAUSAGES, AND SCRIPTS   129
The manufacturing process isn't always fun to watch

Contents

UNITED WE STAND 132
When the Writers Guild invites you in, it's an offer you can't refuse

THE GREAT DIVIDE 137
Staff writers in this camp, freelancers in that

STALWARTS AND PILOTS 140
How do you pick a winner and get on board?

THE BACK DOOR 145
Sometimes the indirect route works best

Part VII: Making Hay

CATCHING A BREAK 153
It's all in what you do with it

OPPORTUNITY IN CHAOS 157
Disorganization can be a writer's best friend

GLORY DAYS 161
A weekly salary is not such a bad thing, after all

Part VIII: Staff Life

AN OFFICE OF ONE'S OWN 169
Make yourself at home, for a while

PLAYING WELL WITH OTHERS 173
Staff meetings can be a bonding exercise, or an exercise in bondage

WE MEET AGAIN 178
Or, what cooperation can accomplish

O Canada!   181
Why you should keep your passport handy

The Beginning of Wisdom   185
How many colors can a script come in?

Earning Your Keep   189
In TV, you don't write—you rewrite

An Inside Job   193
Sure, writers may not be welcome on set, but they're seldom shot

Casting a Wide Net   198
Wait till you see who the casting director brings in

Hard Lesson #1: Shut Up   204
You go along to get along

Hard Lesson #2: Speak Up   207
The meek may inherit the earth, but they'll never make a living in TV

Taking Credit   211
In an arbitration, there's more than you know at stake

Part IX: Endgames

Bad Signs   221
How to tell when the end is near

Heaven, Hell, and Purgatory   226
In a development deal, you can languish in limbo, or win the lottery

Two for the Load   230
Collaborating as a cure for loneliness

Contents

HIRED GUNS   238
What your agent doesn't do for you, a manager might

BETWEEN JOBS   251
Nothing succeeds like the appearance of success

Reading Advisory

The events and actions in this book are based on my own personal experiences and on the first-hand accounts of other TV writers who have confided in me. The only things I've changed are people's names, the titles of some shows, and identifying details here and there, wherever it was appropriate or prudent.

Other than that, it's the unvarnished truth.

▉▉▉ Part I

Slouching Toward Hollywood

Our Hero Arrives

■ ■ ■ If I told you I came to L.A. kicking and screaming, that wouldn't be accurate.

I came to L.A. comatose.

I was living in New York, and I'd been married only a matter of months when Laurie, my *wife* (I hadn't even reached the point where I could say the word without stopping for a second, and thinking, *Wow—I must be married*) announced that she'd quit her job at *Vogue* magazine.

That was headline number one.

Headline number two was even more shocking. We were moving, it seemed, to her hometown. Los Angeles, California.

To be completely honest, the first thought that crossed my stunned mind wasn't, *Los Angeles? Moving? When? In truth, it was, What happens to our health insurance?*

For years I'd been a freelance writer, paying for every antibiotic, every flu shot and X-ray and vaccination out of my own pocket. But once we'd gotten married, I'd qualified for the comprehensive *Vogue* magazine plan, which covered just about every physical mishap you could think of. Before Laurie, I'd been pretty much dealing only with the medical emergencies and letting my overall health concerns slide, but *now*, now that I had *health insurance,* I'd already gone in for a teeth cleaning, an eye exam, a mole check, a migraine consultation, an EEG, an EKG, a CAT scan, and I was giving some serious thought to a triple bypass (why not; it was covered).

But now, suddenly, it looked like all of that—my hopes and dreams for a whole new, bionically healthy me—was shot.

"When did we decide to move to L.A.?" I asked.

"On our second date. I said that I was sick of New York and wanted to move back home, and you said that sounded like a great idea and you'd have no problem living in L.A."

Now it did begin to sound vaguely familiar. But as *I* remember it, back then I was still trying to convince Laurie to fool around with me, and at that point she could have said she wanted to open a trailer park in Kentucky and I'd have said *that* sounded like a great idea to me, too. Anything, just so long as it kept my romantic prospects alive. And no court of law, to my mind, would ever hold against a man something that he'd hastily agreed to on only a second date.

Still . . . she *had* quit her job.

And, as she was explaining now, "I've given the magazine two weeks' notice, and I've told my parents we'll be needing the back bedroom until we can find a place of our own."

A few weeks later, Laurie did indeed move to L.A., with about three overstuffed suitcases of clothes and a batch of hastily Xeroxed résumés. It didn't take me long to notice she was gone—I'm perceptive that way—but it did take me another month or so to wrap up my affairs in Manhattan, and hire Moishe's Movers to come and get the rest of our stuff. On the morning of the move, my younger brother, David, who's like a taller, stronger, nicer version of me, stopped by the apartment and found me wandering like a zombie from room to room, my mouth hanging open, my arms hanging uselessly by my sides.

"Are you okay?" David asked.

"Yes, fine," I said, stumbling over a box of books.

"You don't look fine."

"I'm fine."

He picked up a vial of pills from the kitchen counter. "Elavil?"

"Uh-huh. I took a couple."

And they had apparently hit me—a guy who can get drunk watching a beer commercial—with the force of a sledgehammer. David later told me that my eyes were looking in different directions.

Somehow, with my brother's help, I was able to oversee the loading of all our furniture, the locking up of our overpriced apartment on East 46th Street, and the cab ride to the airport. I saw it as a good omen when the clerk at the American Airlines counter, for reasons I'll never fully understand, handed me a ticket that said Seat 3-A.

Even in my stupor, I knew a first-class seat number when I saw one.

"Excuse me, but much as I'd like to sit in the first-class cabin, I've only got a coach reservation," I explained.

"Not anymore you don't," he said breezily, without looking up from his keyboard.

"But I can't afford a—"

"Don't worry about it, it's just an upgrade. No charge." He waggled his fingers at me, to move me along. "Enjoy your trip." He glanced over my shoulder at the person behind me in line. "Next."

In retrospect, I can only assume that he took pity on a guy whose eyes were looking in two different directions.

On the flight, in the peace and tranquillity of the first-class cabin, comfortably surrounded by my betters, I slept—which was more than I'd done for the past several nights—and awoke only as the plane began its descent. Blearily looking out the window, I saw a smattering of little blue dots, which for a second I thought were raindrops on the glass. But then, as I came to full consciousness, I realized that they were swimming pools glinting in the late afternoon sunlight.

And that's when I knew, without a doubt, that I wasn't living in New York anymore.

The lure of writing for Hollywood certainly didn't hit me immediately, and it's hard to say exactly when it did.

Was it the day I stopped in the parking lot of a trendy store called Fred Segal and saw a script from *The X-Files* lying on the black leather seat of an open Porsche convertible?

Maybe it was the night I attended a Halloween party thrown by a dweeby young guy who wrote for *The Simpsons*, in his two-million-dollar Beverly Hills spread, with black-bottomed pool, gazebo, and guest house.

Or was it the fourteenth time someone innocently asked me, after I'd admitted that I was a writer, "Oh, which show do you write for?"

In New York, if you said you were a writer, it was assumed that you contributed to magazines or newspapers. Perhaps you wrote books. Nobody ever assumed that you were a screenwriter, or that—God forbid—you wrote for television. If you did *that*, you'd never even admit to it. Better to admit that you were a drug dealer or something.

In L.A., the situation was completely reversed. It was like entering an alternate universe. In L.A., writers wrote for TV or the movies, and that was about it. Not only that, nobody held you in contempt for doing so. In fact, if they knew anything about the business, they were generally impressed. Everybody knew the kind of money to be made in TV and movies; bus drivers could cite the weekend box office gross, waitresses could speculate on what the incursion of cable has done to network TV, the gardener could tell you the difference between ratings and shares.

And after a while, even I had to admit that it seemed pretty silly to be in Hollywood, the entertainment capital of the planet, and still be churning out the kind of articles I was doing for places like *Redbook* ("Ten Things Men Don't Know About Love," "Twelve Things Women Don't Know About Men," "Thirteen Things Nobody Knows About Anything"). Hadn't I made my contribution to the world of letters?

Why shouldn't I be writing for television or film? That was the work that was out here, in sunny L.A., my new home, and that was the work that paid for all those Porsches and pools I kept stumbling across.

It seemed increasingly crazy not to just reach out and grab some of that for myself. I mean, I'd watched TV as much as the next guy. How hard, honestly, could it be to write that stuff?

Hubris

██ ██ ██ And that, my friend, was my first mistake.

Don't let it be yours.

Sure, I know, you watch some dreadful sitcom, where the laugh track has been cranked up to the decibel level of a DC-10, and you think, "Geez, was that supposed to be funny? I could write funnier material than that."

Or you stare glassy-eyed at an action/adventure show where things keep exploding for no apparent reason, and you ask yourself, "Is this entertainment? I could do better than that."

And you know what? There's a good chance you could.

But getting there—getting to the point where you know what goes into those sitcom scripts, or TV movies, or one-hour dramas—is harder than you know. Getting to the point where you know how to write and *sell* those scripts is even harder.

And if you approach the job with the wrong attitude—if you come at it thinking the work is going to be a breeze, or that it's beneath your talents somehow, or that you're going to be able to knock it out of the park your first time at bat because, after all, "it's only TV"—then you are probably going to fail.

How do I know this?

Because I meet people all the time, both cocky young writers and embittered older ones, who've foundered for just this reason. And because, if I'm going to be completely honest here, I was guilty of the same offense.

Without going on about it at too great a length, because I know that's not why you're reading this book, I did arrive in L.A. with a certain number of writing credits behind me. Let me just get this over with, because it does serve a purpose.

I'd written countless articles, essays, and reviews for dozens of national magazines and newspapers, including the *Washington Post*, *New York* magazine, *Redbook*, *Omni*, *Town and Country*, *Cosmopolitan*, and so on. I'd contributed a very popular column, called "His," to *Mademoiselle* for six years, and out of it I'd constructed a book called *What Do Men Want from Women?* I'd also written ten other books, ranging from collections of folk wisdom to novels of supernatural suspense.

I don't mention any of this to brag—you'd only have to read the books to see why—but because I want you to understand that I was not exactly new to the writing profession. I'd been at it for years, I thought I'd pretty much established that I could make a living with the written word, and I figured scripts were just going to be another kind of writing that I would eventually learn how to do.

I even thought—and this is how misguided I was—that Hollywood would be glad to have me.

Weren't we always hearing about the dearth of good writers in the entertainment business, and the burgeoning job opportunities?

Wasn't there a whole slew of new shows on the air every fall, and then, once those had failed, another bunch at midseason?

Didn't every TV show have a nice long list of writer/producers that crawled along the bottom of the screen for the first five minutes of each episode? (Incidentally, most of those names listed, executive producer, supervising producer, creative consultant, story editor, are in fact the writing staff. Perhaps the idea of calling someone a mere writer is considered too demeaning.)

I actually thought that the television industry was eagerly

looking for new voices, fresh perspectives, undiscovered talent. At least that's what the studio heads and producers always said in interviews. But as I learned for the umpteenth time—and this is as true in TV as it is in any other arena—people don't always mean what they say.

Storming the Barricades

■■■ Truth be told, the TV business is in many ways a closed system. When you're starting out and trying to break in, you will get that feeling over and over again. At first it feels as if TV is some impregnable fortress whose walls you're trying to vault with a pogo stick and a prayer.

All I want to tell you right now is that you're not crazy. You're not alone. We've all been there, we've all felt that way, and even though I've actually made it inside the fortress to some extent, I still feel like I could be thrown out at any time. By the time you read this book, I might have been. But at least I now know *why* it's so hard to get into the TV writing trade.

The reasons are several.

For starters, there are a lot of people working in TV, writing and producing the shows that we see every day, and many of them are good-hearted, generous folks, who would be only too happy to extend a helping hand to newcomers trying to get into the game. Unfortunately, most of the time, they don't have a hand left to extend.

If these people are currently working themselves, they are probably swamped. Television is a very time-consuming, intensive business. Sitcom writers routinely sit around the table till all hours of the night, eating cold pizza, drinking flat soda, and trying to top each other's punch lines.

Drama writers stare for hours, days, sometimes weeks, at the greaseboards on their office walls, trying to outline all the beats in three separate story arcs, all of which have to fit together, and get neatly resolved, in one hour-long episode.

Even if these people had the inclination, right now they don't have the time to read your sample scripts, or answer your questions, or perform the necessary introductions. Many of them lose touch with their own family members, and only meet them again in divorce court.

And then there are the TV writers who are *not* working. That's another story altogether, but with equally unpromising results. If writers are *not* gainfully employed, they're either too depressed to pick up the phone, or they're out there trying to land their own next job. If they have any favors coming to them from anyone in the industry, they're trying to call them in on their own behalf. The last thing they want to do is use up some of this valuable capital trying to find work for someone else.

And finally, as with almost anything else, there's the money, which creates just one more barrier. If you didn't already know something about the fantastically lucrative wages paid in TV, you probably wouldn't be reading this book at all. You'd be filling out your law school application. In fact, when it comes to the various forms of writing with which you can make a living in this world, most of which I've tried—from journalism to books to advertising, even to feature screenwriting—I doubt there's any kind of writing that pays as well, word for word, as television.

This lesson was brought home to me early on, when I appeared on a writing panel at a local university here in L.A. One of the other panelists was a guy named John, and he was the head writer on what was at the time a hugely popular sitcom. While a few of us were having lunch together in the student center, we started to swap war stories about what it's like to try to make a living as a writer in this world. The poet moaned about the difficulty of landing grants, the journalist complained about magazine wages that haven't risen since the days of F. Scott Fitzgerald, I threw in my two cents' worth on the struggles of the midlist author in a publishing climate increasingly focused on the blockbuster book. And maybe because he was just trying to get into the spirit of the thing—you know, writer as down-trodden wretch—John said, "Try writing for a show like mine."

We all stopped—*Was this an invitation?* The poet was ready to chuck his rhymes, the journalist his leads. I silently swore never to write another book.

"I can't call my life my own," John went on. Mentioning the famously difficult comedienne who was the star of his show, he said, "She expects me to be at her beck and call twenty-four hours a day. She doesn't think anything of calling me on a Sunday morning, a Saturday night, to tell me she thinks the script sucks and she wants me to get the whole thing rewritten. By Monday."

"Wow, that sounds bad," I said in my best impression of sympathy.

"It is, it is," John said.

The other writers clucked and cooed.

"And get this," John said, having found such a responsive audience. "She called me, at my home, on Christmas morning—Christmas morning! To bitch about an act break!"

We all registered shock, horror, and immense distress. The poet, I have to say, gave the best performance of us all. He actually laid a consoling hand on John's sleeve. (*Damn, why didn't I think of that?*)

But it wasn't until the following week, when a newspaper article about the wages in the TV business appeared, that I realized just how vast the gap between us was. "Head writers on sitcoms," the article said in effect, "live at the whim of their sitcom stars." It mentioned John's particular star. "Although her head writer takes home $45,000 a week for his trouble, he'll be lucky to last two seasons in the post."

The article went on, but I didn't. I was stopped, arrested, stunned into immobility. Forty-five thousand a week? I knew he made a lot—why else had I feigned undying friendship?—but $45,000 a week?

My first reaction was amazement, but then I felt numb. How could he have the nerve to complain about *anything* when he was taking home $45,000 a week! She called him at home? On Christmas morning? For that kind of money, he should have been at her house, in the kitchen, basting her turkey. I would have been. I would have been there the night before, too, trimming her tree, setting the table, and if necessary sweeping out the chimney.

But the point had now been made with all the impact it would ever require.

TV pays . . . and very well.

Though most positions fall short of John's (and he was indeed fired when the season ended), you'd still be hard put to find a staff job on a comedy or a drama, for a full season, that didn't pay you somewhere above the six-figure mark. A friend who got her first job on a sitcom staff made $135,000; an acquaintance of mine, a veteran writer on *The X-Files*, was making an annual salary of around $850,000. He never got too specific with me, perhaps for fear that I'd cry.

As for the money you'll make writing individual scripts, there are so many different rates in TV, for network versus cable, sitcoms versus hour-longs, freelance versus staff-written scripts, and so on, that it would take me days to sort through them all for you. The Writers Guild of America puts out a booklet called the "Schedule of Minimums"; it's thirty pages long, filled with charts and tables, and I still can't figure out exactly how much is paid for what.

Just to give you some ballpark figures, so even your fantasies can be grounded in some sort of reality, a half-hour sitcom script would earn you about $18,000. A one-hour drama, about $26,000. A movie-of-the-week, should you be lucky enough to land one of this diminishing breed, approximately $54,000.

TV wages are so good that anyone already inside the club is reluctant to let anyone else—anyone still *outside*—know just *how* good they are. In that respect, TV writers act like members of any exclusive club. They're very reluctant to divulge information about what goes on inside the clubhouse walls, and they're equally reluctant to allow in too many new members.

13

They're particularly reluctant, it may seem, to let in too many new *female* members. I'm often asked if TV is the boys' club it's reputed to be, and much as I'd like to be able to report that it's not, that it's a gender-blind meritocracy where women are just as easily accepted and employed as men, I can't.

In my experience, and the Writers Guild has statistics that bear it out, the overwhelming majority of TV writers and producers are men. Men who hire other men—their golf partners, fraternity buddies, guys they've already worked with on some other staff. On the last three shows where I've worked, for instance, I can tell you that the first show had no women on a writing staff of six, the second had one woman on a writing staff of five, and the third had no women on a writing staff of three. At one of these shows they actually made some noise about the dearth of female writers, and I went to the trouble of bringing in a great spec script from a friend of mine, an experienced writer of the female persuasion who was temporarily out of work. I handed it over to the lone female executive at the production company, since I thought, for obvious reasons, that she'd be the most receptive audience.

She cradled the phone on her shoulder long enough to take the script, along with my hastily mumbled pitch for my friend the writer, and gave me a silent thumbs-up. When I saw this exec a week or two later, it was at a meeting where, among other things, she was announcing the addition of another writer to our overburdened staff—a writer named George. No mention of my friend's script, or the lack of a female point of view on the show, was ever made again.

Aside from the numbers, it's the atmosphere at most shows that declares TV a male universe. It's a grungy, competitive, loud, aggressive, boisterous, locker-room spirit that prevails in the halls, at the staff meetings, in the rough-and-tumble give-and-take at notes sessions. I'm not saying that women couldn't handle it—I am saying that they're seldom given a chance to. More than once when I was on staff, I felt like I was back in second grade, when some friends and I formed a club called the Pirates. There weren't many membership requirements: You had to have a red kerchief to tie around your neck, you had to have a squirt gun, and you had to not be a girl. In TV, some shows—too many shows—are like that.

Which isn't to say women can't get work. *Please* don't let this stop you. But women tend to get their work on certain shows where other women have already cut a path or, better yet, where women are the show's creators, executive producers, or show-runners. At those shows, nothing matters except if you can do the job. At all the others, if you're a woman, you can expect to be the one everyone turns to when they have a question about the strange and foreign world of *emotions*—"What do you think, Miriam, would the little girl cry when her kitten's run over?"—or when the script needs a love scene.

Still, whatever you have to do to get into the TV clubhouse, you should do. It is, admittedly, a hard club to join, and a hard club to stay in, but the benefits once you get there are extraordinary. For boys and girls alike. In fact, if I could think of a way to do it all by myself, I'd bust the place wide open for everyone. The membership rolls need some new blood, if you ask me.

A Friend in the Business

■ ■ ■ And that, in essence, is why I'm writing this book. When I was starting out in TV writing, which, trust me, wasn't very long ago, I had a million questions, about everything from how to pitch a story to how to bind a script. From start to finish, the whole enterprise was a mystery to me.

Fortunately, I had friends in the business, men and women who actually went to studio jobs every day, or wrote scripts from their own home offices, for all kinds of shows. I figured I could go to these pals of mine and find out how this TV business worked, and how I could get in.

Boy, was I ever in for a shock.

For every straight answer, I got twelve obfuscations. Phone calls weren't returned, lunch dates were canceled, promises that were made weren't kept. It was as if these people worked for the CIA, and I was blowing their cover.

A good friend of mine, who had once volunteered to read any sample script I wrote, was astonished one day when I actually did try to give him one. "Anytime you have a chance to look it over," I said, "I'd really appreciate hearing what you think."

As I extended the script, he looked at me with such horror, his hands frozen on the arms of his Eames chair, that there was literally no way I could pass it off to him. I might just as well have been offering him a lab specimen. Thoroughly embarrassed, I simply reached a little to his left and placed the script on a shelf next to his big-screen TV.

A month later, when I went back to his house for a dinner party, I actually saw the script exactly where I'd left it, only partially obscured now beneath the latest issue of *TV Guide* and an empty Diet Pepsi can. We never did discuss it.

What I needed, and what I hope to provide with this book, is the friend in the business that, to be perfectly blunt, I never did find. The one who would tell me just what I needed to know, who would answer any question, no matter how trivial it seemed, with patience and candor, who would, in short, unravel the mystery of television writing and tell me how I could start to do it myself.

Because—and this is definitely worth mentioning right here— you *can* do it. It may take work, it may take perseverance, and you may take some lumps along the way (in fact, it'd be a miracle if you didn't), but if writing for TV is what you really want to do, you'll eventually get there.

Provided, of course, that you do have one thing, and that is . . . a modicum of talent.

Now, you'll notice that I say a *modicum* of talent—not an abundance, not an overwhelming, irrepressible flood, not a veritable Niagara of ideas and inspiration. A modicum will do.

Why?

By answering this question—which nobody asked me to pose in the first place—I will pretty much seal my fate in this town. Not only will I probably never work again, I'm not sure I'll ever be invited out for dinner, or even feel safe leaving my apartment in broad daylight, but it's something I think bears saying, and I do happen to believe it's true.

Not all TV writers are overwhelmingly talented.

There. It's done. The heresy has been uttered.

I've worked for magazines, written for newspapers, all that sort of thing, and I think I have a pretty fair idea of the relative abilities of journalists, novelists, and other subsets of the writing trade. What surprised me the most when I started reading scripts and then, over time, meeting successful television writers in this town was, for want of a better expression, the *modesty* of their gifts.

For one thing, most of them appear to have forgotten, if they ever knew, all about such niceties as grammar, spelling, and punctuation. I have never seen such messy work. One script I read last week, which prominently featured a character named Sergeant Ames, had the word "sergeant" spelled four different ways over the course of just the first act. My own feeling is, if you're not going to be accurate, at least be consistent.

But in this business, that would be considered a petty concern, though I do not agree that it is. To my mind, if you don't have absolute respect, even reverence, for the language and how it can be used to express every nuance of what you want to say, then you should be making your living in some other way altogether.

More to the point, TV writers have, as a group, what I consider to be a fairly weak grasp of the language, and what it can do. Whether they came into this business with faulty skills, or whether they've simply taken one too many beatings from development execs, I can't really say.

Nor would I mention *any* of this if it weren't for the fact that TV writers—again, as a whole, with many notable exceptions— are so mistakenly convinced that their generous paychecks are a reliable indicator of their talents. As someone who writes for TV myself, I'm constantly appalled by the arrogance, disdain, and high-handedness with which TV writers often treat their brothers in arms: journalists, book authors, struggling screenwriters. I think, on some level, TV writers know they're onto an amazingly good thing, and the guilt they feel over raking it in is transmuted into a precarious sense of superiority and rectitude. "Hey, if I'm making all this money, I must be good!"

That might be true.

And it also might not.

•   •   •

Now that I've put my life on the line, let me tell you why I did. I've got two reasons.

One. Don't be cowed by what you hear from TV writers, or what you read about the complex demands of this craft. Yes, it's tricky, and there's a lot to learn, but with that modicum of talent I mentioned, you will succeed. These people you're competing with aren't Proust. Most of 'em aren't even Sidney Sheldon; and don't let them tell you any different.

Two. Don't allow yourself to become one of them, the arrogant and sloppy ones, especially when you're starting out. When I was a staff story editor, I had scripts submitted to me by newcomers who apparently shared with veteran scriptwriters this same cavalier disregard for everything from consistency to spelling.

And guess what? I was very put off. Call me a pedant—plenty of people have—but I felt personally insulted. Anybody can make an occasional mistake—I'm sure that mistakes will crop up in this very book—but blunder after blunder just tells me that the writer doesn't really care. He or she isn't invested enough in the script to put it through Spell-Check, to read it over, or to get things right.

One young writer, when I mentioned this problem to her, actually said, "Well, come on—most of what you're talking about doesn't appear on the screen anyway. Who cares?"

She had a point. I had to sit back and think about it. But when I was done thinking, I did still care, because her lack of attention did *not* limit itself—it never does—to what was left offscreen. It also showed up in more essential matters, like character motivation and believability, which do appear onscreen. Carelessness in one regard inevitably shows up in others. Even if you think you can get away with something less than your best effort, don't do it.

It's your best effort that'll get you where you want to be.

So, What Does It Take to Be a TV Writer?

■ ■ ■ Okay, so now that I've committed the crime of taking TV writers down a peg or two, I'd like to turn around and elevate them again. After all, I don't want you thinking this is going to be too easy.

What do TV writers have? What special gifts or talents? What do they know about writing TV scripts that the novice does not? Lots of things. But perhaps above all, a good TV writer can take the bit between his teeth—*any* bit—and run with it.

As a case in point, I remember a particular script, written by a veteran TV writer named Greg, which was one of the first teleplays to make a big impression on me. Greg had only recently come on board at a show where I was on staff, and one of the producers had assigned him a story idea that I thought was tepid at best. In fact, I remember feeling enormous relief that the idea had fallen on Greg's desk and not mine. I thought it was pretty much a lost cause.

But about eight days later, Greg turned in the script, and he had done wonders with it. He had taken the producer's very simple premise—too simple, I thought—about two characters in a *mano a mano* contest, out in a snowy wilderness, and he had wrung so many changes on the idea that the story never flagged.

He kept finding new ways to up the ante, to place the hero in greater and greater danger, to add mystery to the bad guy and leave us wondering just who or what he really was.

He used his stage directions sparingly but well; he made the story visual; he let it unfold almost before my eyes so that even as I was reading the pages I was seeing the action take place. That, more than anything else, is what distinguishes a good TV script, or screenplay, from any other form of writing. It tells its story in a highly watchable, streamlined manner, with scenes and images—even more than the words—carrying the action forward and holding the interest of the audience. This quality, perhaps more than any other, will set your scripts apart.

Make it visual. Make sure the audience has something interesting to look at. Let's say you have to write a scene in which two characters exchange some vital information. You can do it with both of them standing in one place, on a sidewalk outside an office building. Okay, but what if they could have their little chat while shooting skeet, or playing raquetball—wouldn't that give the scene some life, and the actors something to do?

When the characters do speak, make sure that what they have to say is fresh and distinctive. In addition to conveying the important plot information and moving the story forward, the dialogue must also tell us something about who the characters are. Their dialogue—the choice of words, syntax, and grammar— must reflect their own idiosyncratic personalities. The stevedore shouldn't sound like the secretary. If, for instance, you find that you can easily transpose a speech from one character's mouth into another's, then it's a safe bet that the speech needs to be reworked. Your dialogue must be written in such a way that only one voice, one *character*, could ever utter it convincingly.

Greg's script did all that and more. In fact, I was so impressed with it, but at the same time, so well acquainted with the vagaries of the business, that I actually called him at home that Saturday night, right after I'd finished reading it.

"I don't know what will become of your script once everybody else has read it and given you your notes," I said, "but I just wanted to let you know that, regardless of what they say next week, it's a fantastic piece of work."

Greg was stunned. First of all, TV writers almost never get praise, much less from their fellow staff writers, and on a Saturday night yet. But I believe he was grateful to receive it, especially in light of what happened.

The script was not a hit with the producers. For whatever reason, they didn't like it, or maybe they no longer liked Greg. He was given a raft of notes, many of them unnecessarily harsh, and at some point he was taken off the script altogether.

Another writer, far less talented, was given the same idea. That much I do remember. He went on to execute it (a particularly apt choice of verb) with only a fraction of the imagination and flair Greg had brought to it. This version of the script, however, made it all the way into production and onto the air.

The lesson here?

All you can do is your best work, and let the chips fall where they may. TV is not only a collaborative medium, it's a hierarchical one. Everybody has somebody else above him who can second-guess, overrule, or countermand his decisions. Even Rupert Murdoch has to answer to God.

I knew that much already, and I think that's why I had instinctively made that Saturday night call to Greg. I had no way of knowing how his script would go down with all the other people it had to impress, but I just wanted to be on record as a fan.

I'm still glad I did so.

"And Then What Happens?"

■ ■ ■ In addition to all the things I've already mentioned, what a good TV script has going for it is a strong and compelling story. The audience should always be asking, "What's going to happen next?"

If you're watching a sitcom, you should not only be laughing, but also wondering how things can get any worse for your protagonist. How he's going to get out of the scrape he's in, straighten out the misunderstanding, or put things right again in his own little comic universe.

In a drama, you should be sitting on the edge of your chair, wondering what further complications are going to ensue, making matters more difficult, dangerous, scary, for your hero. What will the verdict be? Will the patient survive? Will the bomb go off before the train leaves the station?

As a writer of comedy or drama, it's not enough to come up with a premise or a setup, no matter how good it is. You've got to keep twisting the knot, changing direction, letting things unfold in surprising and interesting ways, so that your viewers are always waiting for the next plot turn, the next beat. Never forget, those commercial breaks are like gilded invitations to change the channel. Your job, as a TV writer, is to make sure your audience is so involved in the story you're telling them that they'd never even think of hitting the remote.

Or perhaps I should say, the *stories* you're telling. The more you watch TV—especially the good shows, like *E.R.*, *The Practice*, *Ally McBeal*—the more you realize that each episode isn't made up of one story; it's made up of several, and the action cuts back and forth among them.

Not surprisingly, the main story is known as the "A," the secondary storyline is the "B," and sometimes there's even a "C." What this means for you, as a TV writer, is that you have to come up with more than one plot line per episode. If that sounds like a headache, trust me, it's not. It's a much bigger headache *not* to have more than one story line going.

Why?

Because if you just had one, you'd quickly find that your episode is proceeding in much too linear and plodding a fashion. You'd find yourself following one character as he tracked the serial killer or hatched his plan to foil the treacherous office manager and, before you know it, you'd be as bored as your audience.

By having a secondary or even tertiary story line to turn to, you can break up the main action. You can allow a little suspense to hang in the air, or you can leave your viewers worrying; worry, in TV, is a good thing—it means the audience is involved. *Will the lovers get back together? Will the disease prove fatal?* Worry means they'll stick around to find out.

Another story line can also give you the kind of time breaks you might need to make the main plot seem less mechanical. In other words, you don't have to have your serial killer kill again for at least fifteen or twenty minutes. You can cut away to something else, maybe something less grim, so that the pace and the mood of the episode are more varied.

On an even more practical note, a subsidiary story affords you an opportunity to employ other members of the show's standing cast. If two of the doctors in the cast are fighting it out over a lifesaving procedure, two others can be having a romantic spat. That way everybody gets some screen time (and in TV, those cast members are all looking for something to do each week), while providing you with a chance to write some scenes that have different voices, coloration, and tone.

In other words, if you have a pretty heavy A-story, then your B-story can be lighter, more amusing. Your C-story, if you've got one, can be downright quirky and flyweight. When things are really working right, your stories not only add excitement to each other, they amplify and resonate with each other. They can deal with the same theme—lost love, fathers and sons, the inevitable toll that time takes on us all—but do it in different keys, in ways that are subtly integrated and even more subtly complementary. The audience members should never feel like they've been hit over the head, but instead they should feel, at the end of the episode, as if they've explored some idea, even if they couldn't quite tell you right off the top of their head what it was.

I am not saying by any means to make your scripts a learning experience—Yikes! We'd all be in big trouble if you did that. People hate to feel that they're being edified. Unless they're deliberately watching the History Channel, they want to feel confident that when they get up from the sofa, they'll be just as ignorant as they were when they sat down.

Consequently, your first order of business, as always, is to keep your audience entertained. If, in addition to that, you can sneak in some meaningful themes, some subterranean ideas, stuff that might leave your viewers (without them catching on) enlightened, enlarged, intellectually stimulated, then you've really earned your residuals.

Decisions, Decisions

■ ■ ■ Unfortunately, for anyone entering the world of TV writing, there's one big decision that you have to make, pretty early on, and it's kind of like picking your major in college.

Do you want to write comedy or drama? Which is another way of asking: Do you want to write half-hour (comedy) or one-hour (drama)?

If you've already raised your hand with a question—namely, why can't a drama fit into a half-hour format or a comedy last for one full hour?—you've proven yourself to be way too radical, too free-thinking, too rebellious for your own good. If you keep on thinking thoughts like that, the TV police will search you out and have you forcibly removed from Los Angeles County. So watch it.

For the time being, this is just the way it is (with only rare exceptions, such as *Northern Exposure* or *Ally McBeal*, which successfully thwart the categories). Although you may insist that, as a writer, you want the opportunity to be funny *and* serious, to write heart-rending dramas *and* uproarious comedy, you'll simply have to pick one or the other for now, and then, much later on, when you're as rich and famous as David Kelley, you can thumb your nose at the industry dimwits who set things up the way they are, and do what you want.

For now, you must choose. Not only because this is the way the business has been arranged, but because, as an unproven quantity, you will need to work doubly hard to create an identity for yourself, a reputation as a certain kind of writer. You're not doing this for yourself, or your friends, or your family—they all know that you are a multifaceted person of many talents and diverse moods. No, you're doing it for the agents, the producers, the show-runners whom you will have to deal with down the road.

These people don't have time to discover the many dimensions of the real you, and in most cases they don't care to. They need to pigeonhole you, and fast. The agent needs to know who he's selling, the producer needs to know who he's buying. For that reason alone, at the outset you have to pick one category or the other. Otherwise, you risk confusing everyone.

So how do you choose?

Okay, this shouldn't really be that hard. Ask yourself this: what are your three favorite shows on TV? I'm always astonished, in classes I teach, when some of the students can't answer that question. They're taking a class in TV writing, and they can't name even three shows that they like? Why would they want to work in a medium they have so little interest in?

If you don't enjoy TV or watch much of it, then do not attempt to make a living at it. Becoming a TV writer not only requires a certain, preestablished taste for the tube, it also means you're going to have to watch hundreds, and over time thousands, of hours of television, just to keep up with what's on the air from season to season. If the thought of doing that makes your eyes glaze over and your brain snap shut like an excavated clam, get out now, while you still can.

If you *do* have some TV favorites, what are they? Are they comedies or are they dramas?

If they're all one or all the other, we're done. You should be writing what you watch.

If they're a mixed bag, as mine would be, then you have to give it some more thought. You have to make a fair and objective assessment of your talents and proclivities, and base your decision on that. To help you out, I've provided some rough profiles, the kind you might see in an astrology column, of the stereotypical drama and comedy writer.

You're a drama writer if . . . you like to read novels more than short stories, and your tastes run to anything from Anne Rice to Charles Dickens. You enjoy long walks on the beach, in the rain, and when you broke up with your college boyfriend/girlfriend you kept a journal of your suicidal thoughts and profound insights into the nature of human relationships. More than once you've referred to your apartment as a garret, and your walls are hung with Canaletto posters. You're a good listener and remember people's names. One day you plan to put all this TV nonsense behind you and write serious novels.

You're a comedy writer if . . . you would much rather be at a party than at home reading a book. You enjoy late hours, loud clubs, and when you broke up with your college boyfriend/girlfriend you threw up in a paper bag and left it on their doorstep. More than once you've facetiously referred to your apartment as your "crib," "pad," or "love nest," and your walls are covered with Marx Brothers posters. The only reason you ever listen to anyone is to see if they're providing you with a good straight line; and, of course, you don't remember who they are because you never asked their name in the first place. One day you plan to put all this TV nonsense behind you and write serious novels.

If there's one thing that all TV writers seem to share (at least all of them that I've met) it's this secret idea that they're only doing this TV stuff to make a lot of money, and that as soon as they've cashed out, they're going to really put their talents to use and write the big novel that's been fermenting steadily inside them.

Why, it was only yesterday that a TV sitcom hotshot called

to tell me he was very disappointed in *The Shipping News*, which, to his astonishment, had "won the Pulitzer Prize a couple of years ago! Wow," he said scoffingly, "if that book can snag a Pulitzer, it really makes me want to get down to it with my own book. We wrap up our season next month, and I'm going to take a few months to bang out my own novel."

Now, suffice it to say, this guy is in his midforties and to my knowledge has never written a word of published, or publishable, fiction. But that doesn't stop him from thinking of TV, which has brought him a house in Beverly Hills, a garage full of new cars, and a seven-figure investment portfolio (I know this because he never fails to mention such things), as the *impediment* to his true calling.

What can I say? If you really want to write novels, write 'em. But don't kid yourself. Having laboriously constructed three of them myself, I can tell you, it's an altogether different discipline, and though no one in L.A. wants to hear this, it's just plain harder than writing scripts.

Not that scripts are easy.

There are a million different things to think about while writing a TV script, and entire books have already been written to help the neophyte learn how to do it. Semester-long classes are taught at universities, with the sole object of getting the students to turn out one complete script by the end of the term. Degrees are granted in screenwriting.

And while I suppose I could try to do some of that here, I don't really think it would serve any purpose. For one thing, those other books and classes are already available. For another, I'm not sure you can ever really teach the whole process in a book. You really do need to enroll somewhere, even if it's just extension-style classes at UCLA, NYU, or wherever, where you can get some real-live human feedback from, ideally, a good instructor, and from your classmates. An individual response to your material is essential, and, if you do happen to be in a class setting, you need to hear your dialogue spoken, tried out, even if it is only by other writers. You'd be amazed at how much is revealed to you just by hearing what your words sound like when uttered aloud. I once wrote a speech for a character that, after it had been read aloud by the instructor, got a uniformly enthusiastic response from my classmates. Everybody was laughing and saying things like, "What a creep that character is!" "Dead-on! I knew a jerk like that once!" "Boy, have you captured the voice of the classic narcissist or what?"

I tried to accept the acclaim graciously, but inside I was dying. That speech wasn't supposed to be the voice of a classic narcissist or twit. It was supposed to make you *like* the character . . . because the character was *me*! That speech was my heartfelt *cri de coeur*, my *de profundis*, each word wrung like a drop of blood from my very soul. I didn't know whether to strike the speech . . . or kill myself.

But what a book can do, and this one will attempt, is to keep steering you in the right direction, around the reefs and back into the open sea-lanes. In my time, I made a million mistakes that betrayed me as a nonpro, and I don't want you to do the same. I want you to make only your own, original mistakes.

For instance, there's the all-important question of spec (which stands for "speculative") scripts. These are the scripts you're going to write, for free, in order to get other scripts to write, for money.

You know in your bones that you're good, but when you're starting out, you need a spec script or two to make your talents so overwhelmingly and undeniably clear to the writers and producers who still hold the keys to the kingdom that they line up to enlist your services.

■■■ **Part II**

Spec Fever

On Spec

■ ■ ■ Of course, in some ways I'm the worst person to listen to when it comes to advice on writing spec scripts. I hate it, hate it, hate it, and as a result, I've done much less of it than I should have. I'm just ornery that way. If I'm not writing something on contract, for real money, then at least I'm writing something that is all my own, in the hope of selling it to somebody when it's done.

With spec scripts, you're not writing on assignment, and you're not writing something that is totally and forever, for better or worse, your own creation. You're borrowing the characters, setup, and tone from a TV show that's already on the air.

A spec script is strictly an audition piece, a sample of your work designed to show your talents so that someone reading it will say, "Gee, we should hire this person to write for our show!" If you have some secret fond hope, as I once did, that your spec script is going to be so good that the producers immediately embrace it—and you—and decide to actually shoot the thing just as you've written it, forget it. It not only won't happen—it can't. (It's true, I've heard stories of people who wrote spec scripts that were picked up and shot, but I've never actually met the writers who supposedly managed it. I think it's just one of Hollywood's urban legends.)

Why can't it happen?

For one simple, if mind-numbingly stupid, reason: The spec script you write will not be submitted to that particular show. In other words, if you write a spec episode of *NYPD Blue* because you love the show and really feel you know the characters inside out, your agent will send it to *Martial Law*. If you write a *Just Shoot Me* spec, it'll go to *Will and Grace*. If you write a *Buffy the Vampire Slayer*, it will be sent to *Charmed*.

Who thought of this brilliant system? No doubt the same people who keep changing your area code the minute you receive your new stationery.

When one of my old agents first told me to write a spec, I grudgingly agreed to do it. I wrote an episode of *Northern Exposure* in part because it was one of the few shows with which I was reasonably familiar, and in part because it was a critical darling at the time.

Anyway, I took a few weeks off from my regular duties and wrote what I thought, and hoped, was a successful episode. I printed out an extra copy on three-hole punch paper, put two brads in it at the top and bottom (don't put three, by the way—it makes script pages harder to turn), and sent it over to the agency.

And then I waited.

And waited.

And waited.

After making several phone calls over a period of a couple of months, I finally managed to get the agent, Stuart, on the phone, and he told me that yes, he'd read the script, "and it's really good."

Even though I was immensely happy and relieved to hear that, I didn't want to appear too needy, so I just said, "Thanks. I'm glad you liked it."

"Sure."

There was an awkward pause, during which I heard him muttering something to someone else in his office. So I waited silently for him to finish with whomever he was talking to, before going on with our own conversation. Then I realized our own conversation was quite possibly over, so I said, "Great, great. Now what do we do with it?"

"With what?"

"The script. The spec script." I had the distinct impression that he had already forgotten what the call had been about.

"Oh, well, I guess that depends."

"On what?"

"Who do you know in the business?"

It took me a second to process that question. Who did *I* know in the business? At that point I'd been in L.A. for less than a year, and my best connection in the business was the guy who'd installed cable in my apartment. And anyway, Stuart was at one of the hottest talent agencies in Hollywood. Wasn't *he* supposed to know people in the business?

"Well, I don't know that I know anyone. I thought, you being an agent and all, you might know some people we could show it to."

That didn't seem to make a dent. "How about college? Did you go to college with anybody who's on a show now?"

Still stunned at the way this conversation was going, I racked my brain, and the only person I could come up with, who I knew had attended the same university as I had, was David Kelley (at that time most noted as the creator of *Picket Fences*). Not that I knew him. Not that we were even in attendance at the same time.

"Well, David Kelley went to the same college I did, even though I didn't actually know him there."

"That's fantastic! Send him a letter—don't say your agent told you to do it—and tell him you'd like to write for TV, you're a big fan of his work, all that stuff. Then when he gets back in touch, we can send him the spec."

With extreme reluctance, I composed the most charming, modest, undemanding letter I could, sent it to Kelley, and waited again—only this time it was over in a few days. I got a call from Stuart, and he didn't sound pleased.

"Did you send a letter to David Kelley?" he said.

"Yes, just as you suggested."

"Did you tell him I'd put you up to it, that you had a spec script?"

"No, I don't think so—though I did mention that I was represented by you. I thought it made me sound more professional."

"That's *not* what I told you to do! If you're going to get anywhere in this business, you've got to do exactly what I tell you. And I told you not to do that."

"Well, I didn't know what else to say in the letter. It's not as if I was contacting him just so we could hang out together and talk about our old college days. I've never even met him."

"And you won't be. I got a call from his office, and they said he's not reading any specs. So that's it."

"Gosh, I'm sorry, I guess I'll have to do it differently next time. I'm really sorry."

Fortunately, I didn't have to find a way to do it differently the next time. There was no next time, at least not with Stuart. He had already soured on my career prospects.

And I had begun to form an opinion of TV agents.

Maybe you're wondering, *Why don't spec scripts go to the shows that they're episodes of, anyway?* Here's what I was eventually told.

First off, producers and staff writers are very wary about reading spec scripts of their own show. There's always the chance that you'll have written something perilously close to another idea that they're already developing in-house. There's no way you could have known that, of course, but as far as the producers are concerned, there's always the danger that, six months down the line, you'll see an episode that seems suspiciously close to the spec you submitted, and you'll decide to sue. I know, I know, you're thinking *I'd never do that,* but trust me, other people do.

Even more to the point, the writers and producers at any particular show are so well acquainted with the characters, plot points, internal logic, and tone of their show that any outside script, no matter how good, will never make a favorable impression on them. They'll always see the flaws.

But other shows in your favorite show's same general category—like cop shows, doctor shows, sci-fi shows—are considered fair game. You can assume that the writers and producers on this show, the one you would *kill* to write for, are reasonably familiar with other successful shows in their overall category. So if, say, your dream is to work for *The X-Files*, and you want them to read a sample of your work, make your spec script an episode of *Profiler*.

But if you really feel most comfortable writing a spec of *The X-Files*, the show you worship, then go ahead and do it—just understand that the script will probably do you more good at *Farscape* or *The Pretender* than it ever will at *The X-Files*.

Whenever they have any downtime, most TV writers I know are working on a spec—or two or three—in order to keep their skills honed and their portfolio fresh.

What they don't waste their time doing is writing spec *pilots*; neither should you. Writing a spec episode of your own original series idea is, in almost every case, about as useful as attempting to perform cold fusion. Much as you might long to create your own show, a spec pilot stands almost no chance of being read. Even if it's good, it doesn't do what a spec script has to do, which is show off your ability to capture the texture and format of a known, preexisting show.

As a TV writer, *that* is going to be your job. You're going to have to be able to walk into a series that's already on the air, with its own kind of stories, its own set of characters, its own zeitgeist, and compose episodes of the show that fit seamlessly into the pattern established by all the other episodes that have preceded it, and all those that will come after.

Even the best TV episodes do not have any individual writer's stamp upon them. They bear the stamp of the show itself—that's what they're supposed to do.

Meet the Candidates

At any given time, there are perhaps half a dozen shows that are considered, by the industry, to be good spec material. These are not only successful shows with good ratings and all of that, but in most cases they're relatively new. In other words, you probably don't want to invest too much of your time and effort writing a spec episode of a show that might soon run out of steam and get canceled. There is nothing deader than a spec of a show that's no longer on the air. (Would you care for a copy of my spec of *Northern Exposure*?)

Nor do you particularly want to write a spec of a show that has already been done to death by everybody in town. There was a time you couldn't walk down the street without tripping over a *Seinfeld* spec. Before that it was *Cheers*. Right now, it's *Providence* and *The Practice* that are clogging the photocopy machines at Kinko's outlets all over town.

Ideally, what you'd like to pick is a hit show, one that you personally like, that's also generating some heat. With a new show, you have the luxury of knowing pretty much all the episodes that have aired, and yet you can still come up with something that might be fresh. Try *that* with a show that's in its sixth or seventh year.

How do you find out which shows are good prospects? If you have an agent, ask him or her to give you some choices. It's the sort of thing agents are supposed to know.

If you don't have an agent, look at the ratings; read *Variety* and *Hollywood Reporter* to see which shows have been picked up for a second or third season. Look at the covers of *TV Guide* to see which programs they're featuring. It's not really hard to figure out which shows are making noise. Frankly, in L.A. it's sometimes hard to *shut out* the noise.

Once you've picked your target show—let's make one up, a sitcom about a wacky Italian family that runs a diner in New Jersey, and let's call it, say, *The Borgias*—you're ready to start doing the necessary groundwork.

First, tape an episode or two (as many as you can, in fact) of *The Borgias*. And watch them. Carefully. With a legal pad in your lap.

What are you noting on the pad?

For starters, you're noting the story lines. What happens to the family each week? Do they get mixed up in other people's problems—other customers at the diner?—and then use their rough but effective interpersonal skills to help resolve them? Do they get into huge family feuds? What do the various members of the family want—to get out of the restaurant business? to keep the diner going strong for another generation? to sell Mama's marinara sauce to a big faceless corporation and get rich?—and how are they routinely thwarted in their desires?

Jot down in no more than a couple of sentences what the main plot of each episode is about.

Next, make a separate list of the regular cast in the show, divided into the main characters (the leads) and the secondary characters. Who are the Borgias, and how would you describe each one of them, individually? Is Papa the hotheaded patriarch who can't understand why anyone would want to work anywhere outside the diner? Is Mama the long-suffering one, who's also the secret brains behind the operation? Are the kids dying to, respectively, (a) become an FBI agent? (b) get married and move away? and (c) take over the diner and turn it into a national chain?

And how do they interact with the secondary characters in the show—the customers at the diner, the people who live on the lower floor of the Borgias' Weehawken row house, the distant relations who come for a visit?

What you are doing, in essence, is analyzing the components of the show and seeing how they fit together, what makes them work, and, most notably, what makes them funny. With any luck, as you watch each episode, you're absorbing the rhythms of the show, the pace, the way the characters speak to each other. This is the stuff you can't really diagram very well; you've just got to learn to feel it in your bones. In some sense you've got to become . . . a Borgia!

The same procedures, incidentally, hold for a one-hour drama. Study the show until you know it inside out.

But all the watching in the world can only help you so much. The other thing you need is a sample script, and I don't mean your spec. I mean an *actual* script from the show; ideally, an early draft. The later production drafts have all kinds of scene numbers and stuff like that stuck in, which you don't need to worry about; they'll only make the script look more technical and, for a newcomer, more baffling. A first or second draft will show the original writer's intentions more clearly, and in less cluttered pages.

Even though most shows follow the standard formats for one-hour or half-hour scripts, the one thing I've learned is that every show has its own idiosyncrasies of style. Some shows use a longer teaser (the opening scene) than others. Sometimes they actually vary in the number of acts they have. Sometimes scripts for a particular show run a bit longer, or shorter, than the industry average. (On average, it's forty-eight double-spaced pages for a sitcom, and fifty to fifty-five single-spaced pages for a one-hour drama. The rule of thumb is that a page of drama script, or two pages of sitcom, equals one minute of airtime. Commercials fill the rest of the allotted time.) Also, sometimes you can't really tell how a character's name is spelled until you see it written out. Having an actual script in your hand, from the show you're planning to spec, is very handy; it really helps you get yours right.

Once you have a chance to flip back and forth through the pages of the script, you may even find the prospect of writing the spec a bit less daunting. An hour-long script, you'll discover, doesn't contain all that many words. The only trick is picking the right ones.

So how do you get hold of such a rare artifact as a show script?

Again, if you have an agent, it's his job to get you one. If you don't, there are stores that sell them. Just to get you rolling, let me suggest two such places. One is Hollywood Book and Poster Company at 6349 Hollywood Boulevard; they'll sell you a TV script for $10 and a movie script for $15, and you can call them at (213) 465-8764. In the unlikely event that they don't have what you want, you can also try Script City, which will take mail and phone orders at (323) 871-0707. A movie script will run you $19.95 and a TV episodic script $14.95.

If you happen to live in L.A., you can always get a free read by dropping in at the library of the Academy of Motion Picture Arts and Sciences, at 333 South La Cienega Boulevard in Beverly Hills. The phone number there is (310) 247-3020. The only hitch is that even though you can read all you want, you can't make any photocopies.

It's also possible to get a script from the show itself, though it rather depends on who answers the phone when you finally get through to the right production office. Put on your best phone manner, plead without being too pathetic (you don't want them thinking you're a nut case) and offer to send whoever it is you get on the phone a stamped, self-addressed envelope in which to mail the script back to you. You might even mail this underling, as thanks, a box of chocolates or a Blockbuster gift certificate. I am told, though I have fortunately never had to employ this direct-appeal method myself, that it generally works.

If you can't get a sample script, just employ the standard one-hour or half-hour script formats that are outlined in any standard screenplay-formatting book or software; if you just follow the ordinary rules, you won't wander too far afield or advertise in any way that you're new to the game.

As for which software to use—and you'd better use one brand or another, or you'll go out of your mind indenting, setting margins, breaking speeches, and so on—it doesn't really matter much.

Personally, I use a program called ScriptThing, which is fairly popular, and which does everything I can imagine needing a program to do. But the last two shows I wrote for used, respectively, Scriptware and a later program called Scriptware Tagged. Still, the disparity wasn't a problem, because when I was done writing my script in ScriptThing, I simply followed the instructions in my manual and converted it to the programs used by the other two shows.

For the record, you will always be expected to turn in the scripts you're assigned on a disk, formatted to the script program employed by that particular show. And more often than not, you'll also be asked to send along a printed-out hard copy; I send one along even if they don't ask. That way the staff at the show can check the old-fashioned way to make sure that they've got all the pages and text—before, of course, they start rewriting every word.

Not that your spec script will ever *be* rewritten; specs, remember, are just audition pieces, which either get you the job or don't.

However, you may decide, of your own volition, to rewrite your spec. You may want to rewrite it because it doesn't seem to be making much of an impression on agents or producers. You may want to rewrite it because an important cast member has just quit (say, George Clooney leaving *E.R.*) . . . or the show has taken a radical turn of direction . . . or you just saw a plot nearly identical to yours on that week's episode.

None of these things would spell absolute doom for your script—after all, it is just a spec, and it's understood that, not being on staff, you could not have been privy to any big changes that the show had in the works—but some things do leave the script feeling dated. And dated is not an impression you want to give. (I once wrote a spec in which two of the main characters danced around the subject of becoming engaged, but by the time I was done with it, on the show they'd gotten married and she'd become pregnant.)

Unless you're a mind reader, or you have an inside source at the show, there's no avoiding some of these traps. It's just one of the things that makes writing for TV such a wild and madcap ride.

A good spec script is a mixture of the bold and the cautious, the innovative and the tried-and-true.

On the bold side, you want to write a script that is "out there," that wakes up producers who read it, that comes up with something—plot turns, jokes, new wrinkles in the fabric of the show—that demonstrates you can take a proven product and add something to it, a sparkle or zest or approach that is fresh and your own.

On the other hand, you don't want to be so original and surprising that your spec no longer reads like the show it's supposed to be an episode of. To that end, there are certain things you should definitely avoid.

Do not, for instance, write a spec script that requires a lot of new and expensive sets; producers who read your spec will want to know that you understand the budget exigencies of TV. When I was starting out, I made that mistake on a couple of the scripts I was first assigned, throwing in big crowd scenes and lots of different locations. One of the show's producers, who was not my friend, always liked to point out this problem I had in group story conferences. Then he'd explain it to everyone by adding, "Robert, of course, is a novelist," in the same tone you might say, "Robert, of course, has lupus." He was just one of those TV writers who could never forgive me for writing books.

Another thing to avoid is too great a reliance on guest characters. You may absolutely fall in love with your creation, the itinerant peddler full of lessons in life, or the mischievous kid with a sad secret, but if you let your spec revolve too much around this character, who's never been seen on the show before and who would never be seen again, then you've hobbled your script as a selling tool.

Remember, a spec is an example of the show as it *already exists*, meant to show how you can handle its characters, tone, dialogue. The best specs are the ones that hone in on the regular cast members, capture their voices, and find a different and interesting source of conflict between a couple of them. If you can put two or three of the regulars into a new situation, one that calls for real drama or finds laughs in a fresh arena (no, not a real arena—remember what I said about budgets?), then you've accomplished the most important feat of all. You've shown the readers of your spec that you know how to take a series to a new place, and that particular talent, to any producer worth his salt, is an extremely valuable one.

All right, let's assume that you now have written a brilliant spec script. You're on the five-yard line, ready to score; don't fumble the ball now.

Print out your script on clean white paper (I wouldn't mention this if it weren't for the fact that I've seen specs on green, yellow, and pale blue); put a front page on it that gives the title, neatly centered. Below that, put "An Episode of [the show]," and below that, "Written by [your name]."

Do not, no matter how tempted you are, slip in an epigraph from Flaubert, Faulkner, or Jean-Paul Sartre. In a town like this, rife with intellectual insecurity (and for good reason), this quotation would only be seen as a form of one-upmanship and make the readers hate you.

If you feel like it, you can put a date on the lower right-hand corner (so long as you remember to regularly *up*date it) and a line that says, "Registered: WGAw." The latter indicates that you have paid twenty dollars to the Writers Guild of America West to copyright the material; the guild, in other words, has taken your twenty, slapped the script into an envelope, and sent it off to some vast warehouse in a barren waste, where they promise to keep it for five years before throwing it in a furnace to provide heat for the workers who will be warehousing all the new scripts that have arrived that day. It's up to you whether you actually want to *do* this with your spec or simply *indicate* that you did it without truly spending the twenty bucks. Or you can forget it altogether. To be honest, I think the registered line looks a little dorky, especially on a spec, and I'd probably skip it.

Finally, you may, or may not, wish to put two blank cardboard covers, in some innocuous color (a pale gray or blue is fine), on the front and back of the script. I do; I think it keeps it clean and fresher-looking as it makes the rounds. But regardless of what some overeager counter clerk at the copy center tells you, do not go to the trouble or added expense of printing anything like the title and author on the cardboard cover. That's a dead giveaway of amateur status.

Leave your spec looking as coolly professional and laid-back as you are.

Great Ex-Spec-Tations

■ ■ ■ Today is the first day of the rest of your life. The sun is shining through the billowing curtains of your bedroom, birds are chirping in the trees, the smog has shifted overnight to another part of town.

And you have *a finished spec*, flawlessly printed between its cardboard covers, just waiting for the world to sit up and take notice.

So why isn't the phone ringing?

Getting your work into the right hands (getting it read at all) remains one of the most persistent and galling problems in Hollywood.

At least in the publishing world, which I sometimes still inhabit, there's always the "over the transom" route. When all else fails, you can just mail your manuscript to a publishing house and hope some hardworking young grunt rescues it from the slush pile. It's a last resort, true, but it is a resort.

In the TV business, there is no slush pile. You can't just mail your script to a studio or show; they won't read it, for legal reasons alone. It's an increasingly litigious world we live in, and nowhere is the paranoia higher than here in L.A. If you did just mail it in, you'd either get it back with a form letter explaining that they don't read unsolicited material or you'd simply never hear anything at all.

Once, when I was very foolish and untutored, I found myself in a TV office talking to a friend who worked as a PA (production assistant) there, and when she left me to run a quick errand I realized that I was staring at a wall of mail slots for all the producers, writers, and execs at this very successful company. Coincidentally, I had a spec script, hot from the copy shop, in my briefcase.

Thinking this was my one chance to slip in the back door, I grabbed a piece of paper, scrawled what I thought was a pretty winning note to a particularly prominent producer, and stuck the script, with the note attached, in his mail slot before my friend got back. (I in no way implicated her in my crime.)

For crime it was. And the upshot is, I suppose, exactly what I should have expected. Nothing. I never heard a peep from anyone about the script, and, to make matters even more annoying, I couldn't very well ask them to return it. Three bucks in copy and cardboard costs down the drain.

With other friends I have been, I'm very sorry to say, more direct. Sorry for them, sorry for me.

After a couple of years in L.A., I did indeed have a few friends in the business. (After a couple of years in L.A., if you don't have a few friends in the business, you're not getting out of the house very much.) And I did turn to them for help.

First there was Ari, a senior writer/producer on a network show. We met for lunch, where he returned my spec script to me with a big smile and said, "Keep it up."

"Keep what up?"

"Doing good work like this. Two more years, and I'll bet anything you get an assignment somewhere." Then he ordered the Cobb salad, dressing on the side, and spoke no more about it.

Then there was Hal. His wife and mine went to college together, and the four of us had often gone to dinner, until I mentioned that I wanted to get into TV and asked if he'd be willing to read a spec. Hal instantly agreed, told me to drop it off at his office (which I did) and then never again mentioned it to me.

Come to think of it, we don't go out to dinner anymore, either. (Gee, how bad was that script?)

Or there's Sam. Even though I suspected he was using me to pay off a previous favor himself, I went along with it; he'd arranged for me to meet, at the Farmers Market, a writer/producer who was a friend of his. This guy, it seemed, wanted to write a book, and I was the guy who knew how.

"It's a good excuse for you two to meet," Sam said, "and who knows, maybe he can throw some work your way. He did it for me once." (Ah, there was the favor I suspected was being repaid.)

At the market, his friend Larry was as amiable as could be, peppering me with questions about the publishing business, literary agents, book contracts, book signings, book sales. Then, when we walked back to our cars, he took from his trunk a ski boots box, which contained the manuscript he was hoping I could read and critique for him.

"I can't thank you enough," he said, "but hey, if you ever want to get into this crazy TV business, though I don't know why you'd want to, all you have to do is say the word."

Tempted as I was, I didn't say the word—not then, not there. I figured the first thing I should do was read his manuscript and give him my advice, and *then*, once *he* was in *my* debt, admit that I was hoping to get into TV.

Well, I took the book home and read it—and it was dreadful. It was a tract really, not a book at all, about the shocking—*shocking!*—lack of values in Hollywood, with Larry featured as a searcher for a higher truth and more noble way of life.

But I've taught writing long enough, and been at it myself, to know how to give someone even the worst news in a gentle, encouraging manner, which, I swear to you, is precisely what I did. I praised every single thing that halfway worked in the book and tried explaining the exigencies of publishing, how this book could be reworked to make it a more viable commercial property, and so on. Larry was having none of it. As soon as he realized I was never going to get to the part where I tell him I'd already sent it on to my publisher and that his generous advance check was already on its way back from New York, this spiritual seeker went off like a Roman candle.

"Are these *notes* you're giving me?" he suddenly asked, using the term for comments you get on a script from a network honcho. "You're giving me notes?"

"Well, I wouldn't call them notes," I said, backpedaling as fast as I could. The phone grew hot in my hand. "I mean, I'm only trying to help you get the book to the—"

"Listen, I get notes all the time, on every script I do, and the last thing I need from *you* is notes—on my *book*. That's not why I gave it to you. This isn't some script that's gonna go through a dozen drafts—this is a book. It is what it is, and I want it published exactly the way I wrote it. I'm not going to change a word. Send it back to me."

Needless to say, I did. I couldn't get it out of my apartment fast enough, and somehow, after that, I never felt it was a good time to call him up and ask for that help getting into TV. I'm perceptive that way.

Why do I tell you all this? Is it because I'm petty, small, and wanted to settle some scores?

Yes. Never underestimate the long-lasting energy of a grudge.

It's also to demonstrate a point. You must go to your friends, you must go to anyone who has any connection to the business, because that's still (when it works) the most direct route into the business.

And even though most of the time it does not work, you've got to keep trying, nonetheless, because it can eventually click, and it did, as I'll explain later, even for me.

Papering the Town

■ ■ ■ And while you're at it, badgering your friends and neighbors, don't stop there. Be even more profligate with your favors. Put your work in the hands of anyone and everyone—from the secretary down the hall to the woman you met in traffic school who's temping at DreamWorks—who says they're willing to read it.

You never know who will wind up offering you that critical assistance, and the chances are, it's the person you least expect to get it from. (Though I won't belabor the point, some recently conducted sociological studies—and I'm not making this up—have revealed that when it comes to career boosts and assistance, most people got much more help from their *acquaintances*, people whom they knew just slightly, than they did from their good friends.)

Now, a lot of people subscribe to a quite different school of thought. They're very protective, even secretive, about their work. They don't go handing out their scripts to just anyone; in fact, unless they feel there's a very good reason to let a particular person see it, the script stays in the drawer, even if it's only a spec TV episode. That's how afraid they are that their work will be stolen, their ideas pirated.

And Lord knows, I understand their hesitation, especially given the sort of people you meet while peddling your wares in Hollywood. But it's still a terrible idea.

If you keep your work safely in the drawer, that's where it will safely stay—forever. It definitely won't be stolen from you, you'll never have to worry about suing some industry bigwig, and even if you spot some similar idea in a new movie or TV show, you'll have the comfort of knowing it's coincidence and not intellectual property theft.

But you won't get anywhere, either.

You have to take your chances, and put your scripts into circulation, whenever and wherever you can. And you must accept that there is a kind of cultural zeitgeist, a spirit of the age, in which certain ideas and stories are swirling around and taking various shapes. Many writers are reading the same major newspapers and magazines, they're watching the same news stories unfold on TV, they're witnessing, even taking part in, the same trends. And perhaps like you, many of them are trying to guess what the next big thing is going to be, where and when the next big wave is going to break. Sometimes their guess will be the same as yours.

I distinctly remember a bookcase filled with spec scripts that stood outside a studio office I once had. When I should have been working on my own episodes, I often took a break and went out and thumbed through the forlorn, abandoned scripts crammed into the case. Some of the scripts were dreadful, and some were surprisingly good, but what they all shared, every one of them, was a marked resemblance to some high-profile film from the last five or ten years.

One, you could see, was a version of *Twister*, about a group of tornado trackers; one was about a dinosaur island project gone terribly awry; more of them than I could count focused on serial killers in the manner of *Se7en* and *Silence of the Lambs*. And though I never actually went to the trouble of checking the dates on the scripts against the release dates of the famous feature films they resembled, I'm sure they weren't all knockoffs. They were just the also-rans, the versions of these stories and ideas that had fallen by the wayside, or that had indeed been trampled underfoot by Michael Crichton and Steven Spielberg. Not stolen, not pirated, just preempted.

It happens sometimes, and you have to accept it.

By and large, the studios and producers to whom you try to sell your work will behave in a decent fashion—not necessarily because they're honorable (though I suppose it's possible), but because this, too, is in their long-term economic interest.

Face it. If you come in with what they think is a sensational idea, they can try to steal it. No question. But they can also buy it from you, for what to them is a nominal sum, and thereby guarantee that they won't be hearing from your lawyers somewhere down the road, *after* they've inescapably committed themselves to a studio, a budget, stars, and all that.

If they buy it from you and do the right thing, they can also turn around while the ink is still wet on your contracts, fire you off the project, and bring in the people they'd been planning to work with all along anyway.

Behaving in this underhanded sort of fashion might cause *you* to lose sleep, but most producers, believe me, would not find it a hardship. For some of them, in fact, there's no greater joy than knowing that they've managed to take serious advantage of a writer. It just satisfies some primordial urge in them, as would building a fire in the cave or clubbing their own dinner to death. The first freelance TV job I ever had was from a New York producer named Max. He called me up and offered me the chance to write a one-hour pilot for a well-known magician who was trying to get his own show going.

"I need the script next week," he said, then added with an evil chuckle, "and I'm only going to pay you $5,000 for the whole thing."

Now, if Max had known that I had just finished an extensively researched newspaper piece for $750, he might not have gloated quite so much.

"You know why I'm only going to pay you $5,000?" he went on.

"No," I said, already counting the money, "why?"

"Because I know I can get you for that."

I didn't have the heart to tell him that he could have had me for $4,000—or less. He was savoring the moment too much. To add what I could to his enjoyment, I tried to sound displeased. "Well, just how much work is this going to be?" I grumbled.

"I need an intro, I need three short stories—kind of like that old *Night Gallery* show—and I need stuff to go in between and connect 'em."

As soon as my phone was safely back in its cradle, I let out a whoop of joy and danced around the tiny space in my apartment that was officially designated, for income tax purposes, the office.

Then I panicked. At this point, though I'd written for talk shows and such, I had never actually written a script per se, where actors, in costumes, on sets, were going to have to speak lines. My lines.

Fortunately, I did have a friend, Linda, who lived two blocks away and had written several screenplays. So as soon as I had blundered my way through a draft of what I thought a script should look like, I ran to her place, with a legal pad in hand, for her notes and comments. And Linda, a consummate craftswoman, showed me with a few deft strokes how to streamline the action, trim the dialogue, and eliminate unnecessary characters.

Example: In one of the few explicit instructions he'd given me, Max had said that for budget reasons I could not use more than one or two extras in any of the stories, but in the first story, I had one too many. I didn't see who I could drop, until Linda took one look at the script, crossed out the judge, and replaced him with a shot of a gavel falling and a voice-over rendering the sentence. Who needed to actually *see* the judge? All we needed was to hear his verdict. It was as if a veil had fallen from before my eyes. Her way was better, easier, cheaper. That was the moment, I think, that I first realized writing for TV was a whole different ball of wax, with a million different tricks and techniques that distinguished it from any other kind of writing.

I knew I had a lot to learn.

But for a measly five thousand bucks, what'd Max expect?

Part III

Agents of Influence

Secret Agent Man

■ ■ ■ Now, all of your friends in the business of course have agents, but sometimes prying the name of that agent out of them is tantamount to pulling a toenail.

Their agent is their own secret weapon, procured at great personal cost, and they're damned if they're going to part with that information easily. Or jeopardize it in any way by recommending someone—even you—who might (a) prove unworthy, thereby throwing their own taste into question, or (b) prove to be *too* worthy, so talented that the agent is now inclined to work harder on your behalf than he is on theirs.

One friend of mine, to whom I turned when I was anxious to look at scripts just so I could get used to the form, grudgingly sent me one of his, but only after he'd ripped off the title page, which happened to contain his all-important agent information.

Still, it's worth a shot; once you've got your spec in hand, you can ask your pals for a recommendation to their agent. Some of them, just to get out of reading your spec themselves, will agree. This *is* one way to slightly improve your chances of getting the script read and responded to; in your cover letter, just say that so-and-so is a friend of yours, that she has always spoken highly of her agent, and that as a result you have asked for—and received—her permission to get in touch. But unless your friend has in fact read and praised your script, I'd strongly advise against saying anything that indicates her opinion of the material. That would not be quite kosher.

(Unbeknownst to me, one young writer actually called my agent, claiming to be not only a close friend of mine, but someone whose work I hugely admired. His first mistake, which my agent quickly pointed out to him, was that he'd mispronounced my name.)

Finally, you can go the strictly professional, no-special-connections route. Even if you're not yet a member, you can call the agency department at the Writers Guild of America (323-782-4502) and ask them for their agency list, comprising a roster of agents, from all across America, who are willing to read new material from unrepresented writers. The guild will send it to you for $2.50; or, if you have more time than money, you can drive to the WGA headquarters at 7000 West Third Street, Los Angeles, CA 90048, and pick it up for just $1.00. Don't feel like leaving home? You can check out the list on the WGA Web site: www.wga.org.

As a service to my readers—both of you—I had the guild send me the current list so I could see what you get for your investment. It's pink, eight pages long, and it lists nearly three hundred agencies, but the bad news is, only a handful of them indicate that they'll even consider new writers. The worse news is, many of those that *will* consider newcomers are not in L.A., not even in New York, and frankly, once you get beyond those two poles, almost everyplace in between is useless. (Don't blame me! I didn't make the rules, I'm just telling you how the game is played.) Proximity is essential. You need to know your agent is schmoozing with the Hollywood players, the ones who can actually hire writers and hand out assignments, and that's tough to do from Paducah.

Still, the list is useful as a starting point. Many of the agencies on it *will* read a letter of inquiry, in which you can introduce yourself and briefly describe the material you'd like to submit. Don't send anything more than that; you'll be lucky if they even read and respond favorably to your query.

Other agencies will consider you if you can get that all-important referral from one of their current clients, or from somebody they know of, such as Speilberg or Ovitz or Bochco. If you don't already know any of these guys, try to meet one.

Why am I making such a big deal out of this? So what if you don't have an agent?

Unfortunately, because it is a big deal. The way things are done out here, the way the business is structured and run, you must have an agent. Without one, it'd be like trying to eat Jell-O with a fork; sure, it can be done, but it's more trouble than it's worth.

"You Think *Your* Agent Is Bad?"

■ ■ ■ Among the favorite pastimes of TV writers, right up there with rotisserie league baseball and taking afternoon naps, is kvetching about your agent.

It's true that I have two rich and successful friends in TV, who have nothing but kind words to say about their agents. (But let's see what they have to say if their careers ever hit a snag.) Everybody else I know regards their agent as a costly nuisance at best, a festering boil at worst. Most of the time, I lean toward the boil school of thought, but I'll try to maintain some journalistic objectivity.

What is an agent, and why must you let one into your life?

The greatest minds, for several generations, have wrestled with this question, but the inescapable conclusion remains: it's how things are done out here.

Without an agent, you look like a neophyte.

With an agent, you look like a professional.

Without an agent, you are unprotected.

With an agent, you are covered (sort of).

Without an agent, you have almost no way of knowing what's going on inside the business.

With an agent, you have an inside line, in theory, to the latest developments in the television landscape—what's been canceled, what's been picked up for another season, who's now running what show.

Without an agent, you have no one to turn to for career advice and counsel.

With an agent, you have someone knowledgeable about the industry, who has a vested interest in your success.

Without an agent, you keep 100 percent of the money you manage to earn.

With an agent, you keep just 90 percent.

But as even the most innumerate of us can see, 90 percent of something is better than 100 percent of nothing.

As a result, "Who's your agent?" is probably the single most-asked question in L.A., coming right before "Are those real?"

A few weeks ago, I called a car service to take me to the airport, and the driver asked me who my agent was. When I told him, he glanced at me in the rearview mirror and said, "Yeah, I worked with him, too, back when he was at the Morris office."

Everyone in L.A. either has an agent or is trying to get one. The agency terrain is always changing, one place gaining stature, another one declining, so anything I have to say on the subject right now might have changed a bit by the time you're reading this; still, I doubt it will have altered that much.

So, just to give you some idea of the lay of the land, let me say that the three most venerable, big-name, well-known agencies in town are ICM (International Creative Management), CAA (Creative Artists Agency), and William Morris.

ICM occupies what was once a bank headquarters or some such thing on Wilshire Boulevard, and the place still looks a little like that, a sleek, cold fortress of glass and stone, behind a moat-like fountain.

CAA is also on Wilshire, at a busy intersection near the Peninsula Hotel (which the agents use as a lounge). It's got the chicest design (by I. M. Pei) and the lobby, always bustling with stylishly attired people under the age of forty, is dominated by a huge Roy Lichtenstein.

Agents of Influence

William Morris is a block away from Wilshire, on a quieter street. There's a certain comforting staidness about the place—the black leather chairs in the reception area, though in perfect condition, feel like they've accommodated many impressive and accomplished bottoms over the years.

All three—no surprise—are in Beverly Hills.

If you say you're represented by an agent at one of these three, it's a little like saying you went to an Ivy League college. There's a status and recognition factor attached to the agency name, and it rubs off on you. Rightly or wrongly, producers can assume that you've been vetted.

At the same time, there are a host of smaller agencies—often called "boutique" agencies—that are hot, highly reputable, and in some cases more aggressive than their larger counterparts. I have several friends, for instance, who are repped by a place called Broder, Kurland, Webb & Uffner, and they contend that it's an especially great place for TV writers. But if I were a betting man, I'd put my money on Endeavor to become the next colossus. Founded just a few years ago by a bunch of young, renegade ICM agents, it's always in the headlines in the trades (as *Daily Variety* and the *Hollywood Reporter* are often referred to) for signing new high-profile clients, making innovative deals, putting together some lucrative package. Right now it has the heat.

But does it matter, I'm often asked when I teach or lecture, if you're at a small agency or a powerhouse?

There are advantages and disadvantages to each. The big and better-known agencies do have clout; their names carry weight, their agents tend to be veterans, and they have an extensive roster of clients, to whom they can more easily introduce you and your work. It's all about networking, and it's to the agency's benefit if they can load up the TV writing staffs with lots of their own clients. Therefore they do make some effort to connect you to their other, already placed writers and producers.

The boutiques don't have as many clients, or as extensive a web for you to exploit, as the big agencies do. But many of my friends who are represented by these smaller agencies contend that they give you more attention—you're a bigger fish in a smaller pond. The smaller agencies are able to keep closer tabs on you, and they work harder—maybe even more expertly—on your behalf. And when a job opportunity somewhere *does* come up, they'll work very hard to help you—and only you—land it. The big agencies may send over spec scripts from a dozen of their writers and, to be honest, they don't really care all that much which one of their clients ultimately lands the job, as long as one of them does. The smaller agency, having entered only you in the race, cares very much that you win.

So where am I in all this? Let's just say that I am, at present, an insignificant cog in a relatively well-known agency machine. But to better make my points throughout the remainder of this book, I'm going to invent a literary composite, a fictional agency that we'll use to demonstrate so many of the common practices in this industry, and so many of the lessons I've had to learn in this town. Let's give this agency the initials EGO, and per industry standard, leave out the periods that should fall after each initial. What do the letters stand for? Envy, Greed, and Ostentation, the three pillars on which so much of Hollywood proudly stands.

But I got in through the back door, as it were. (Just don't let this get around.) For several years, I'd been represented in New York by a very powerful and immensely competent literary agent, and when I moved out to L.A., I was still her client. Her name had such clout that several of the EGO agents met with me. Each one of them, I think, concluded that I was signed—that is, contractually tied—to one of the others at the agency. Not that it really mattered that much which one of them it was; if you're with the agency, you're with the agency. And even though at some point I recognized their mistake, I'm afraid I never corrected it.

God, I believe, will forgive me.

Anyway, with the respectability her name gave me, I was able to call upon the services, over the years, of several agents at EGO, but I wish I could tell you it was more fruitful than it was. To be blunt, in all the years I've worked with the various TV and movie agents at EGO, they have seldom found me a writing assignment or staff job. And when I ask around among my TV friends, I find, in almost every instance, that their agents—at whatever agency—have done little or nothing for them, either.

Whether my friends are at one of the Big Three, or at one of the smaller boutiques, the one thing you hear, quite clearly, over and over again, from newcomers as well as TV veterans, is that you have to do it yourself. The legwork. The networking. The calling. The spec scripts. For every agent who has actually landed his client a job—a job that the client would not otherwise, on his own, have found or won—there are twenty who do nothing more than field a few phone calls from prospects that the writer himself has unearthed, and then process the paperwork that follows. And yes, they still get 10 percent for their troubles, as the law allows.

If you meet up with an agent who tries to charge you more, do your best to get him to validate your parking before you *run* from his office—because that's the last time you should clap eyes on him.

One of my agents, who has since left EGO for even greener and more lucrative pastures, once professed to me that he never read scripts, and looking around his barren, Japanese-style office (a rock, a white sliding screen, a tiny bonsai tree on the otherwise empty glass desk) I could believe it. There wasn't a scrap of paper anywhere to be seen.

At the time, it didn't trouble me all that much, as I had just landed (on my own, of course) a staff job. It did come back to me a year later, however, when this same agent sent me a contract with the usual Post-it notes all over it, pointing out where my signature was required. Glancing over the contract before signing it (which is always, may I say, a good idea), I noticed that the fee for this TV script was for some reason about ten thousand dollars less than it had been for the four previous episodes of the same show. I immediately called his office, and he cavalierly explained, "I never read contracts."

That's funny, it occurred to me, *I thought it was scripts he didn't read.*

"Just send it back," he said. "We'll take care of it."

I'll give him that much—he did call the show and got the figure corrected, new contracts issued. But I never quite got over the idea that he didn't read scripts, and he didn't read contracts . . . so what exactly was I paying him for? What in fact did he do all day? How much watering can a bonsai tree take?

• • •

I could tell you a dozen stories like this—any TV writer could do the same—but I think the point has been sufficiently made. While you do need an agent, your career rests in your own hands. You can't count on an agent, even a good one, to do for you what you have to do for yourself. Sure, the agent makes 10 percent of your income, and that's supposed to be your insurance that he'll be out there beating the bushes on your behalf, but don't forget, he's got a lot of people like you, a lot of bushes to beat, and as far as he's concerned, it's all a numbers game, where volume counts more than anything. Even if some of his clients aren't raking in the bucks, plenty of others are. The chances that he'll fall behind on his Mercedes payments are slim.

You, on the other hand, have only you working for you. There's no one else on the planet—not even your mother—to whom your future, your career, your hopes and dreams, mean more than they do to you.

While there are things an agent can and should do for you, things that you cannot do for yourself, there are many more that you must help him—even *force* him, if need be—to do for you.

Booster Shots

■ ■ ■ ■ The first thing an agent can do for you is read your spec, love your spec, and figure out what to do with it. That means, he knows who to send it to—not just an address, not just an office, but a *person*, someone who will read it, and who's in a position to do something with it.

Half the battle, maybe more, is getting your material into the right, and most effective, hands. If your script comes into a show at too low a level, there are too many people it will have to go through. For example, a reader or development exec simply might not like it; a staff writer might actually be threatened by its merit. All it takes is one such person to bottleneck you and your work.

A good agent will have a connection high enough up on the totem pole to get your work read responsibly and within a reasonable time frame. Assuming your work gets a favorable reception, a good agent will also be able to arrange a meeting for you with the people in charge—the people who can hand out free-lance assignments or, better yet, staff positions.

In a sense, your agent should be your cheerleader, bandying your name around town, pumping up your stock, promoting you and your work at every opportunity. He should be the one to say all the wonderful things about you and your abilities that you, because you were so well brought up, cannot say about yourself. What modesty prevents you from claiming on your own behalf the agent should be shouting all over the place.

You'll often hear about something called "heat" in this town; all it means is that someone, or some property, is getting a lot of attention, activity, buzz. I wouldn't say I've ever generated what would properly be called "heat," but for a couple of weeks now and then, I have been warm. Maybe even toasty. Twice I wrote books that sparked interest in various quarters all at once, and once I wrote a spec feature that had several producers calling; option offers and deal memos were suddenly floating around. It's the agent's job to capitalize on that temporary—and believe me, it is temporary—rise in your temperature and to nail down some kind of a deal for you before it all dissipates.

A good agent is also a kind of astrologer or prophet. He's supposed to know not only what's happening in the business right now, but what's going to happen in the near future. He should live with one ear to the ground, so that he can hear which shows are going to be canceled, which ones are going to be renewed, and which pilots (premier episodes of new shows) are going to fly. He should know who the personnel are at each of these shows and in their respective development offices, and he should have the clout and connections to get you in those doors to pitch your own ideas.

Finally, and in some ways this is the most important thing of all, a good agent should return your phone calls. It may seem impossibly petty to fret over, but more writers I know have exploded or switched agents over the issue of unreturned phone calls than just about anything else. Sure, agents are busy—an agent's daily phone log is a frightening thing to behold—but as far as I'm concerned, that's still no excuse. It's what headsets and secretaries were designed for. On the one hand, you can't be crazy and expect the agent to pick up the phone right away every time you call, but on the other, if he doesn't return your calls within, say, twenty-four hours, then he's not doing his job. And, if you have the courage, you should tell him so.

Because I generally lack the courage to confront anyone (one of the many secrets of my success), I often send my agent a fax or an E-mail. Friends of mine think this is a terrible idea. But rather than just leaving a message with his secretary and then waiting by the phone to tell him my news or ask him my question when he calls back, I put it all down—names, details, dates, whatever he needs to know if he's going to give me an answer. That way, he's aware of why I'm calling when I do get through, and I have something in front of me—my copy of the message— to refer to. I have an embarrassing tendency to blather on the phone, to work so hard at being affable and easygoing that I forget to mention half the things I meant to bring up. Having that printout or fax in front of me is the best way I know of to make sure that I remember every question I wanted to ask and every bit of business I wanted to address.

Does it work? Do I always get my concerns cleared up and my questions answered?

No, but at least I'm not kicking myself afterward for forgetting to tell him that I'm now living in a cardboard box and that, if it's at all possible, I'd like to work again one day.

The Dotted Line

Most of the time, to be honest, writers are so happy to find an agent who wants to work with them that they never even stop to think, *Do I want to work with this agent?*

But it is something to think about.

Some writers, and for a while I was one of them, make the mistake of thinking that their agent is somehow supposed to be their friend. A pal. The kind of person they'd have as a roommate, or go to a ball game with. Maybe even someone with whom they share some fundamental values and interests.

But that betrays a basic, bedrock misapprehension.

While agents and writers may resemble each other physiologically, I'm convinced that they actually share only as much DNA as humans do with chimpanzees. (Mating, in fact, should be strongly discouraged.)

Writers are creative but often solitary creatures; agents, though outgoing and garrulous, are about as creative as planks.

Writers are introspective and riddled with groundless self-doubt; agents are supremely confident for no reason whatsoever, and the only doubts that ever plague them involve their hair or their sunglasses.

Writers dress in a variety of styles, ranging from intentionally retro to unintentionally retro; agents shop at tony stores and have personal dressers who help them find just the right, au courant items.

Writers like to read books; agents like to read menus.

So, instead of looking for a soulmate, writers should look for agents who *complement* their own personalities, who give them the social skills, assertiveness, optimism that they may lack. All you really have to find in an agent is a decent level of rapport. Even if the agent's vocabulary is limited, is it still sufficient for him to understand what you're saying? Is he courteous to you, does he hear you out, does he do what you need him to do (e.g., when a producer wants to see a copy of your script, does the agent get it over to him in a timely manner)?

If you expect him to remember your birthday, you'd better be *X-Files* creator Chris Carter.

And remember this: Ask not what your agent can do for you, ask what you can do for your agent. If you've gone to a party and met someone who just so happens to be a show-runner, let your agent know about it, especially if that new acquaintance has shown a willingness to read your material.

If you've seen a small item in *Variety* about a new show that's right up your alley, tell your agent that, too, and see if he can arrange for you to meet the people putting the show together.

And keep your agent supplied with live ammunition in the form of new, fresh scripts. He needs stuff to show, and he needs stuff to sell, whether it's a spec TV episode or a feature-length screenplay. Even articles, essays, books can serve a purpose. I've had meetings, and even gotten jobs, based not on scripts I'd written, but on other published materials that were right on target. When a show called *Cupid* came along, I got a meeting with the show-runners because for six years I'd been the love and romance columnist at *Mademoiselle* magazine.

Did it get me an assignment?

By golly, no, it did not. But it might have, if the show hadn't swiftly failed of its own accord.

•   •   •

Customarily, once you and an agent decide to work together, you sign papers with that agency. I say customarily because I've been at both a big agency and a smaller boutique, and through one oversight or another, I never signed papers, as such, with either one.

Please, don't tell.

At the smaller place, I had the feeling they didn't want to be bothered with paperwork until they'd figured out whether or not I was going to make any money for them. This is sometimes called being a "pocket client"; the agency hasn't technically taken you on, but they will allow you to act as if they have; and, in the event of a deal, they'll certainly take their cut. They might then let you join their official roster. As it turned out, I never did manage to climb out of their pocket and onto the team.

Although I had come to them with an actual deal in hand, an offer for a romantic comedy, they managed to so bungle the whole negotiation that I wound up with nothing. In brief, a start-up company had offered me $7,500 to develop the "high-concept" I had pitched them. ("High-concept" simply means an idea so strong and simple and commercial that even a child or development executive could instantly understand it.) The agent, an aggressive young man, scoffed at the meager sum I'd been offered.

"Seventy-five hundred? Are they kidding? Let's go out with this and get some real money."

In no time, he had put me into a deal with a fairly successful producer, who offered me three times that amount. By Hollywood standards, still no big deal, but by mine, a definite improvement, until I realized, as the weeks went by, and I took meeting after meeting with the producer's slow-witted development exec, that we weren't making any progress. At one point, the exec complained that part of the problem was that I hadn't taken the intensive three-day Story Structure course taught by screenwriting guru Robert McKee; the exec was a graduate and loved using the McKee terminology, like "inciting incident" and "progressive complications," and he felt that until I'd taken the class we wouldn't be on the same wavelength.

So I enrolled, for $395. And I did enjoy, and do recommend,

the course, but even after I'd graduated, the project kept stalling. No matter what I did, no matter how many outlines I turned in, no matter how much I'd improved upon my inciting incident or complications, nothing was ever decided upon.

And . . . I wasn't getting paid.

Eventually, I discovered that there *was* a method to this apparent madness. While the development exec kept me tied up in knots, the producer was shopping the idea around town for free. When he didn't get a bite, he—and his deal—simply evaporated.

Cut, as they say out here, to the agent's office, where I— baffled, weary, and out the cost of the Story Structure course— plaintively asked, "What happened to my deal? Where's my money?"

To which the aggressive, but now curiously unconcerned, young agent replied, "You've got the deal memo in writing. Sue him for the money."

"Sue him? Is that how I'm supposed to start my career out here—by suing a producer who's probably got half a dozen lawyers on retainer already?"

"I would."

"Can't we just go back to that company I came in here with, and take their original offer? The seventy-five hundred dollars?"

The agent whistled and rolled his eyes. "I don't think so— not after the way I blew them out of the water."

"How *did* you blow them out of the water?"

"Let's just say it was bad. If I were you," he said, rather proudly, "I wouldn't go near those people again. They hate you."

Somehow, the issue of actually signing papers with that agency didn't come up again. On the way out—without the original deal, the bigger deal, or even a halfway viable project anymore—I took a generous handful of mints from the bowl on the reception desk. I knew it would be all I ever got out of them.

In most cases, however, as soon as an agency decides to take you or your project on, they'll ask you to sign on the dotted line with them. The length of the contract can vary, and although one year is standard, two years isn't unusual. The idea is, it takes time for an agent to get you out there, to get your material read, and for firm offers to materialize.

The agent's cut is 10 percent, and the agency, which receives the checks on your behalf, will also take out all the necessary taxes, then send you their own check for the remainder. Don't be surprised when the gross amount on the check and the net amount (what you actually get) are vastly different. I remember how ecstatic I was when I landed a staff job that paid the princely sum of $3,750 a week—and how stunned I was when the first check arrived for less than $1,700. Yes, the money is wonderful, but wouldn't it be great if you could keep it?

When it comes to residuals (the money you receive for re-runs), no agency commission will be taken; that money is funneled to the Writers Guild, which in turn passes it along to you— and Uncle Sam.

At the end of the term of the agency contract, if things are going well, you'll both want to renew it. Why mess with a good thing? And if things aren't going well, neither one of you will probably be too eager to re-up . . . so again, there's no problem.

Troubled Times

■■■ Aside from everything I've already said about agents—you need them if you want to be taken seriously in this town, you need them to give you access, you need them to keep you clued in, and so forth—you need them the most when something goes wrong.

And something will always go wrong.

It would be wonderful if everyone in this world behaved in a decent and honorable fashion, but, as I'm sure you're aware, they don't. And unless you happen to be one of those people who's ready, willing, and able to stand up for his rights and fight to defend them at every turn, it is very easy to be cheated, duped, tortured, or swindled in this business.

I've been all of the above, and more. That's why I know I must never be without representation—and fierce representation at that. Since I am, by nature, a lamb, I try to enlist the help of a lion.

The first agent I had who *was* that lion—or lioness, in this instance—was my New York literary agent. Editors cowered before her, publishers quaked. As each deal was being negotiated, I had to assure these quivering minions that I understood their fears, that I would rein in the agent if need be, that I too was concerned she might exact too high a price for my services. Of course, after each of these discussions, I would call the agent and thank her again, profusely, for holding their feet to the fire. (My own impulse would have been to *wash* their feet for them.) She was the firm and forceful voice I needed, who said for me what I was afraid to say, or demand, for myself. And incidentally, she still is.

Time and again, my agent demonstrated for me her absolutely crucial role as a buffer and a go-between. An agent is a mediator of sorts, between you and what in essence is your adversary, because, make no mistake, in any business proposition, an essentially adversarial situation will arise.

TV is no exception. The studio, the show, its producers all want to extract from you the best work, and the most work that they can, and for the least amount of money. Sure, the Writers Guild rules prevent them from getting away with everything they'd like, but that doesn't stop them from trying to make the occasional end run; they'll ask for one more draft than they are contractually entitled to, they'll call an extensive rewrite a mere polish, they'll drag you through fourteen story conferences for an episode that they can't quite nail down, and then pull the plug on it altogether.

All of these scenarios have happened to me, and each time I've called upon my agent to pick up the cudgels for me. For example, once when I was on staff at one show, my paychecks mysteriously stopped coming for several weeks. It turned out, the show (shot up in Canada) was on hiatus, the actors and production staff had dispersed to various vacation spots, and no one, I guess, had thought to tell me. Foolishly, I'd kept right on working on script outlines and second drafts, faxing them into the office, until it dawned on me I was getting even less response than usual.

When the puzzle was finally cleared up, the show tried to get out of paying me for the (unannounced) vacation weeks, and I was understandably miffed that (a) I had been working when I didn't need to be and (b) I had missed my own chance to get out of town on a real vacation. But here, once again, I revealed my wormlike tendencies by declaring to my TV agent in L.A.

that the show should pay me for at least *half* of the time I'd spent working.

"What are you talking about?" he said. "They're going to pay you for the whole time."

While that seemed in one sense right and fair, I had already come to feel on some subconscious level that this was all my fault. *How could I have been so stupid? How could I have been unaware that when the show shut down, I was supposed to shut down with it? Why weren't the producers charging me for using up all their fax paper while they were sunbathing in Hawaii?*

The agent in this case did go to bat for me (after all, it was his money on the line, too), the executives did agree to do the right thing (and to notify me in future of such scheduling events), and I was able to put the money aside for the vacation I never did take. For once I was glad that I *had* been paying an agent that 10 percent of my salary.

If the agent isn't there to take the heat when a fire blazes up, then he's not serving one of his most important purposes. You're the writer, and you should never have to put out the flames yourself. You have to maintain a working relationship with the producers of whatever show you're writing for, and you cannot afford to have your relationship with them sullied by these volatile issues and problems, which inevitably arise, again and again.

Fortunately, one of the many rare and wonderful things about Hollywood is that even the worst feuds that have gone on for years are generally set aside at some point. On one show where I worked, the producer hated one writer so much he called him up at 6:15 in the morning, shouted a string of epithets at him, and fired him before the writer even had a chance to sit up in bed.

The next season, lo and behold, I noticed that same writer had written a couple of new episodes for that same producer. Was I surprised? Not really. Once all the hollering and posturing is done, a show still has to get written and produced, and strange bedfellows often meet up again.

So when a problem arises, remember, it's your agent, not you, who's supposed to throw his body into the line of fire. If he's at all reluctant to do so, push him.

■ ■ ■ ■ **Part IV**

Pitching to Win

Perfect Pitch

■ ■ ■ Okay. Let's say your spec is terrific, and your agent has managed to get it to the right producer, who was suitably impressed. The producer wants you to come in for a meeting and pitch him some episode ideas.

What do you do?

Since your spec was undoubtedly not an episode of this particular producer's show but of some other, it's time to start boning up on the show you'll be pitching to. First stop? Again, it's back to your agent. If he's on the ball, he's already arranged for you to receive a packet of information about the show. The packet should contain everything from a tape or two, to a show bible (the overall summary of the show and its current season), to a sample script. He might even be able to give you some directions and advice on what the show is looking to do now, such as focusing more on one character or another, becoming lighter or darker in tone, getting broader or more restrained.

And assuming that the show is on the air right now, of course you're going to watch it, very carefully. Watching will let you see and hear the actors delivering their lines, which is the best way—the only way, I think—to really capture their voices, their inflections, even their relationships to each other. Do they josh? speak from the heart? argue?

Pitching to Win

By taping the show you'll be able to watch it over and over again, until you're completely comfortable with its rhythm, feel, and atmosphere. When it comes time to write, you're going to know instinctively if something sounds and feels like it belongs in the show or not.

It's only by reading the script (or scripts), and by studying that show bible, that you'll be able to see where the show has been, what kind of stories it's currently doing, even where it might be going.

In a way, it's the same process you went through when you wrote your spec scripts. You studied those shows, then tried to figure out a good, solid story idea that they *could* have done, but hadn't. Only this time you're one step closer (one very big and important step closer) to actually getting an assignment. Your spec script was like the audition, and now you've passed that. The upcoming pitch session is going to be your chance to shine.

Prepare yourself for the heavy lifting. You've done your homework, you know as much about the show as any mortal not on staff can be expected to know, and now you need to come up with something to pitch.

Normally, you're given anywhere from a few days to a couple of weeks between the time you're invited to pitch and the day you're actually expected to show up and do it. You don't want to rush things and go in *too* soon, before you've really prepared. Opportunities like this are not that easy to come by (as you well know), and you want to be sure that you've made the most of it.

However, you certainly don't want to take so long getting your ideas together that the producers forget why they were excited about you in the first place. Memory banks in Hollywood are cleaned out regularly, and you don't want to be part of the stuff that gets discarded. Personally, I feel that four or five days is more than enough time to get yourself in gear and come up with some salable material.

Remember, what you're preparing is not an elaborate game plan, not a thoroughly-worked-out-in-every-detail outline, not an actual script or anything even close to it, but just a few ideas. Stories. Don't work yourself into a frenzy over it. Don't second-guess yourself to death. Just sit back, close your eyes, think of all you now know about the show, and try to visualize scenes, ideas, setups for episodes you haven't seen but that you'd *like* to see. That's key. Imagine yourself to be a loyal viewer of that show and try to think of episodes you'd eagerly tune in to watch.

If it's a sitcom, think about what you'd like to see the lead character doing. Would you like to see him finally find the gumption to stand up to his overbearing boss—and what would be the consequences? Or suppose the female lead reads a magazine article on make-overs and decides she needs a total overhaul—what could (and must) go awry? Does she panic? change her mind? go through with it and wind up as someone she hardly recognizes? What are some of the scenes, bits, actions, that would naturally follow from your main premise?

If it's an hour-long drama, it's the same drill, but your premise must be just that much stronger and more challenging; not only because it's got to carry the viewers twice the distance, but because hour-longs must also, by their very nature, go deeper into the conflicts and emotion. (Which is not to say that there aren't sitcoms that do a far better job of plumbing the depths of the human condition than many of their dramatic counterparts. Plenty of them do.)

What you're looking for, in terms of the pitch, are a handful of stories—three is about right—that are easily and succinctly told in a line or two. You might try to come up with a good "logline" for each—the one-sentence summary that would run in *TV Guide*. "Al and Marjorie both decide to run for mayor of the town." "Sergeant Jones must take control of a hostage situation—only to find his wife is one of the hostages." "The Timewarp Team has twenty-four hours to thwart a future dictator who will unleash World War III."

When I was pitching to a sci-fi show called *Sliders*, I led off by telling the producers about an episode idea I was calling "Lindisfarne," after the tiny isle where, during the Dark Ages, a colony of monks worked to preserve and record the gospels. Suppose, I said, our heroes slid into an alternate world where just such a community was working to preserve the accumulated knowledge of mankind against the imminent invasion of alien vandals, and only the Sliders could help them succeed?

"We'll take it," the show-runner said, the moment I'd finished. Which was, of course, what I'd been fervently hoping to hear. But it was also, forgive the immodesty, what I thought I had a good chance of hearing. After studying the show, I'd realized that what they liked were stories that had a mythic or historic feel, a resonance if you will, and the Lindisfarne idea not only had that, but it was original; I hadn't seen, or read a synopsis of, any episode in which this particular notion had been explored.

I had also done something else. Having decided upon the overall high-concept, the adventure/exploit element of the show, I had then addressed the personal drama question: whose story was it? How would the various leads come into conflict with each other or with members of the isolated community on this isle? What would they learn, or how would they change? And what, finally, would the resolution of the episode be, in terms of both the adventure story (in this case the alien raiders conquered the community, but not before the community's work had been spirited out by two young survivors), and in terms of the personal/emotional stories (one of the leads helped a teenage boy to resolve his difficulties with his father; another found herself tempted to abandon her fellow Sliders and stay in the seemingly peaceful isle)?

TV episodes, whether sitcom or drama, must work on both of those levels, always. They must tell a fresh and engaging story, with plot turns and surprises and snappy dialogue, but they must also address some deeper, core issues relating directly to the characters. By the end of the episode, the viewers must have learned or seen something new about one of the principals.

To be perfectly honest, that's where I usually fell down on the job. I didn't have much trouble coming up with high-concept story ideas, but I was regularly beaten over the head by producers for paying more attention to the big exploit than to the emotional moments that the actors would need, and want, to play. If you want your pitch to fly, by all means come up with the big idea, but in the very next breath address the characters and make it very clear how this story will affect, change, involve them.

During that same pitch session at *Sliders*, I was asked if I had a second idea. I did, of course, and I pitched it—but this one was too close to something they were already working on.

"Any others?" one of the younger producers asked.

I pitched a third, and this one fell fairly flat.

"Anything else?" he asked, but none too enthusiastically.

And even though I was so overprepared that I did have a fourth, and even a fifth, idea in my kit bag, I decided to fold my hand and leave with my winnings. I still had them hooked on that Lindisfarne idea. If you sell even one idea in a pitch session, it's a huge victory! I didn't want to drain any more of the excitement for me, or that idea, out of the room.

It's like knowing when to leave the party, and that time I did it right. All the way home from Burbank, I was pounding the steering wheel with joy, singing along with the Kinks ("Lola," if you must know), and figuring out how to spend my residuals.

This, of course, before I'd actually written a word of the outline, much less the episode. Like most writers, I was never happier than when I had a writing assignment but I wasn't actually writing it.

Inside Information

■ ■ ■ Strange as it may seem, one way to come up with original pitch ideas, ideas that you alone are likely to come up with, is actually to think for a second about things you know about (jobs you've had, subjects you've studied, people you've met) and see if somehow they can be made to fit into or fill out a potential episode. Sometimes these little things can give you a leg up, a small advantage in the great game of landing an episode assignment.

Case in point: When a producer for *Early Edition*, the light-hearted drama set in Chicago, called to see if I had any ideas, I immediately cast my mind back to the days when I was growing up in suburban Chicago. What did I know about, or remember, that someone who wasn't from Chicago might not know? One of the first things to surface, one of my fondest memories, was the annual school outing to the Field Museum of Natural History to see the mummy collection.

Knowing that the producer also hailed from the Chicago area, and that the show already had a built-in supernatural bent, I said, "Have you ever thought of doing something with the mummy collection at the Field Museum?" Before I could even go on, he laughed and said, "No—but that's a great idea!"

"Yes," I said, leaping to embrace his enthusiasm, "suppose a mummy exhibit causes a curse to fall on the city, and only Gary [the hero of the show] can stop it?"

Over the phone, I threw out a couple of other half-baked (quarter-baked?) ideas before I realized it would be better to shut up, regroup, think the idea through, and then make a more formal, worked-out presentation in person.

We set a date for early the next week, and I spent the whole weekend reading up on ancient Egyptian burial practices, looking at photos from the famous traveling Treasures of Tut exhibition, and watching the old Boris Karloff movie *The Mummy*. Then, once I felt I had a good handle on that aspect of the setup, I sat down and figured out some ways in which the leads on the show could be made to interact with the mummy story, including the ways in which they could be put into direct jeopardy.

As I've confessed, that's where I need to force myself to concentrate. While it's nice to have your heroes involved in someone else's problem or crisis, if the heroes themselves don't wind up in some direct danger themselves, you've missed your big chance. Agents Mulder and Scully don't just walk into town and clear up an X-file. Instead they get thrust into the action, the menace redounds on them directly, Scully gets an alien implant in her neck or Mulder swallows an invisible water monster.

Keep your leads front and center, and whether it's a drama or a comedy, make sure that they have at least as much at stake, if not a good deal more, than anyone else onscreen. In a drama, what might be at stake is their very lives; in a comedy, it's more likely to be their reputation or dignity. (Will Jerry Seinfeld have to wear the asinine "puffy shirt" on national TV?)

Strange as it may sound, you should *want* your audience to squirm a bit on behalf of your leads. Audiences like it. They want to be caught up in the predicaments of their favorite characters, and they trust you, the writer, to get the characters back to a safe harbor by the end of the episode. They expect you to give the episode a satisfactory wrap-up—even if that wrap-up indicates that the story line will continue the next week.

If you've done a good job, they'll be eagerly awaiting the next installment.

The Windup

■■■ If you're expecting fashion advice about what to wear to a pitch meeting, I'd recommend you wear something you're comfortable in—but not your pajamas. Dress the way you would if you were going to a nice dinner at a friend's house on a Saturday night.

One of the first times I was invited in to pitch (for a job writing monologues for a TV variety show), I didn't know any better, and I actually pulled out my dark blue pin-striped suit, the one normally reserved for bar mitzvahs and weddings.

After I'd done the interview and pitched my jokes and comedy ideas, I got home, selected some workaday clothes from the tidy pile on the floor of my closet, and waited by the phone, which rang an hour later. It was one of the producers, the one in fact who had suggested me for the job in the first place.

"They can't make up their minds, and they want to see you again," she said.

"How come? Didn't they like my material?"

"They liked the material fine. It was you they didn't get."

"Pardon me?" I did a quick rundown in my mind—I'd shaved, I'd showered, I'd applied a dash of masculine cologne, perhaps too much? "What didn't they get?"

"The executive producer said he did think that you were funny—"

"That's good, that's what we wanted."

"—but he couldn't get past the suit. He said you looked like a Philadelphia banker."

Is that what bankers looked like? In the course of my life, I've been mistaken for everything from a maitre d' to a vagrant, but never before a banker. Still, I was prepared to accept the verdict. "So, what should I do?" I asked.

"Come in again tomorrow, same time. And for God's sake, lose the suit."

I did. The next day, I showed up wearing a sweater, chinos, clean sneakers. And this time, the EP—who was dressed, as he had been the day before, in a Wisconsin sweatshirt and jeans—not only laughed at my jokes, but gave me the thumbs-up for the job. Now, it seems, I not only talked like a writer, I *looked* like one!

I hope this goes without saying, but it's a good idea to show up on time—not so early that you look like somebody with nothing better to do than sit around the lobby, but by no means late. If the office or studio you're going to is fairly distant, or you don't know the geography, study a map the night before. Since I am congenitally incapable of reading a map, I have to beg my long-suffering wife, Laurie, to write out explicit directions on a legal pad for me. "Turn left at the Unocal Station. Go two blocks, turn right. Park at the first meter you see. Put in coins. Take sidewalk to door. Open door. . . ." You get the idea.

On those rare occasions when Laurie's been out of town or otherwise unavailable to provide me with written instructions, I've actually plotted out the course myself, to the best of my limited abilities, and then done a trial run. The day before I'm due somewhere, I follow the exact route I'm planning to take and see how long it takes for me to get where I'm going. (*Please* don't tell Laurie I do this—she thinks I'm strange enough as it is.) It generally takes me longer than most people to get anyplace in L.A. because I take what are called "surface streets"—known elsewhere simply as streets—rather than the much faster, but frequently confusing, freeways. I have a tendency to daydream while I drive, and if I'm on a freeway it's entirely too easy for me to wake up again only when I'm stopped at the border crossing to Tijuana.

On ordinary streets, I can stay awake and alert—and be at my best when I finally get to the studio gate . . . and the production office itself.

In the ten minutes or so you sit in the reception area before being called in to do your pitch, you can spend the time in one of two ways.

You can sit very still, concentrating on what you're going to say, entering the zone, as it were . . .

. . . or you can do just a little more "homework."

I vote for the homework.

Most of these reception areas are alike—copies of the trades on a coffee table, a couple of unobjectionable sofas or chairs, walls festooned with posters from the company's other productions. Sometimes it's amazing what you can learn about the people you're pitching to, just from looking at those posters.

At one place, I quickly surmised that every show they did, besides the one I was there to pitch to, featured a studly hero who seldom spoke, allied with a powerful machine. When I went in to do my pitch, let's just say I incorporated those elements into my own stories.

At another place, where I had *failed* to study the posters, I was pitching to an exec who kept suggesting one particular comedian for the main role in my story, and I kept batting the suggestion aside on various grounds—the comic was too old, too limited in his appeal, too uncharismatic, that sort of thing. It was only when we took a break, and I passed through the reception area again on the way to the men's room, that I noticed nearly all the posters featured shows or movies in which this comedian had appeared.

"That's interesting," I said to the receptionist. "So-and-so appears in almost everything you guys do."

"Of course he does," she said, as if speaking to someone who was seriously learning-impaired. "This is his management company."

Needless to say, I had an entirely different estimation of the comedian's talent when the meeting resumed—now, he was not only perennially young, he was also unlimited in his appeal, and brimming over with charisma! Unfortunately, by then it was way too late.

Lesson number one: Do your homework ahead of time, and know as much as you can about where you're going and who you'll be talking to. If it's a studio or production company, find out what else they do—what movies, what shows. If you know who's going to be in the room, make some inquiries; check their previous credits in the Writers Guild directory, for instance.

Lesson number two: If you've got a few minutes to kill before the meeting, and you're done with the posters, chat up the receptionist. It's not only a good way to relax a little, but you'd be astonished at how much you can learn from just a little idle chatter with even a low-level employee. At one production company deep in the bowels of Culver City, I watched as the comely receptionist made endless chitchat with a big, bearded guy in a sweat-stained purple T-shirt who'd just emerged from the vending machine area with a case of Dr. Pepper in his arms.

When he waddled away, I said, "Boy, are you that nice to all the vendors?"

"Vendors?" she said. "Oh no, I don't have time for them at all."

"But what about that guy in the purple shirt?"

"He's not a vendor!" she said, taken aback. "He's the president of the company."

This fact was confirmed for me five minutes later, when I was shown into his office for my meeting and offered one of the Dr. Peppers. At least I knew enough now not to register any surprise.

Keep in mind, too, that the receptionist may also turn out to be the person who'll route your calls or log in your scripts in the future.

If the receptionist offers you a bottle of water before your meeting, take it. Even if you don't need it now, you will in just a few minutes.

The Pitch

■ ■ ■ All right, let me set the scene for you.

Your average pitch session falls somewhere between a job interview and the Spanish Inquisition.

You're called into the room, where you'll find the hot seat—the chair you're going to occupy—and several others, which are probably filled with two or three staff writers and producers on the show. (I've never encountered more.)

The producer who brought you into the show in the first place will introduce you around. Nervous as you may be, do try to catch their first names. Next he'll compliment you on whatever got you this far—the quality of your spec, the recommendation from some other writer, or your close and personal connection to the network head's wife. This producer is the person who will lead the meeting, and to whom you should pay the closest attention.

The others in the room are a mixed lot. While it's possible the staff writers wish you well and want you to succeed, it's also possible that on some level, which even they don't wish to acknowledge, they wish you would spontaneously combust. Most TV writers have secured their positions at great personal cost, and they're a notoriously insecure lot. And now, here you are, pitching to *their* show, and taking the very bread out of their mouths!

What? you say. *How could that be? You're not there for a staff job. You're just pitching to land an episode.*

True. But for every episode written by a freelancer, that's one less episode to be written by a staff member. And even staff members, drawing a weekly salary, are paid extra for each episode they write. So let's just say, in all candor, that they're ambivalent about your prospects.

Still, their boss has brought you in, and since at least one or two episodes have to be handed out to freelancers every season (it's a Writers Guild rule), they might as well give you the benefit of the doubt and hear what you've got.

So what *do* you say?

Take your cues from the room.

There's always an obligatory five or ten minutes of chitchat—*where are you from? what else have you been writing? where'd you go to school?*—before the producer who called you in clears his throat and starts to get down to business.

"So, what have you got for us?" he asks, and now it's time for you to show your hand.

TV writers all do this part differently. Some launch into their material cold, with no notes in hand; some clutch a sheaf of papers nervously and read their pitch right off the paper. Some are born performers, moving around the room; others sit very still and sweat so profusely they get stuck to the chair. These finer points you'll have to work out on your own.

From my own experience, here's what I think works best. I do have a written pitch—no more than one single-spaced page—for each idea. While I'm pitching it, I keep that page in my lap, not because I'm reading from it (that, I think, is a very bad idea) and not because I don't know the pitch backward and forward (by this time I could recite it in my sleep) but because I like the crutch. Once when I was pitching, a guy took a phone call in the room, right behind me, and even though he *thought* he was speaking softly, it wasn't softly enough to keep from distracting me and the others in the room; without the sheet in front of me I'd have lost my train of thought, for sure.

While I'm talking, I try to keep a couple of things in mind. Eye contact is one—you want to draw these people in and keep their attention. (One more reason *not* to read your pitch off the page.) When you don't look people in the eye, it's easy for you to come off as personally shifty and at the same time uncertain about your material.

Uncertainty is one vibe you definitely *don't* want to give off. I can't tell you the number of times, when I was on the other side of the desk, a writer started off his pitch by saying, "I don't know about this idea, it may not be right for your show, I just thought of it late last night, but . . ." By this time he had already sabotaged the idea so effectively, it would have had to be a masterpiece just to break through at all.

Sell your idea. Be enthusiastic about it. You don't have to claim it's the best idea the show has ever heard—in fact, that would obviously not be wise—but do get behind it and allow the producers in the room to feel your excitement and your eagerness to write it. You ever notice how when someone is smiling at you, you're inclined to smile back? Or how when someone yawns, it makes you want to yawn, too?

Take a lesson from that. Make your energy contagious in that same way.

And you should *listen* to the room. When you've finished with your first pitch (and this should probably take no more than five or ten minutes, fifteen at most) you'll either get a polite turndown—"I'm afraid we have something too similar in the works," "Thanks, but it's probably too wild for our audience," "We're looking for stories that are a little more contained"—*or* you'll see a spark of interest in the room.

That spark is yours to fan.

Usually, if an idea is going over, there'll be a brief silence in the room when you finish telling it. Even though everyone may know that it's a great idea, the staff writers in the room won't want to commit themselves to an opinion until they've heard what their superior thinks. Once he or she starts, they'll all chime in.

Seldom do you get a "Fantastic! We'll buy it!" response. But what you do get is measured praise, followed immediately by a question or two. "So do you think it should be clear to Patricia, early on, that she's being framed?" "How would you end it—with George and Martha on the outs, or with them reconciled?" "What about the dog?"

The longer the interrogation, the greater the interest. And while it's nice if you have solid answers to most of the questions, don't sweat it if you don't. The staff members are asking because they don't have answers, either. And no pitch was ever bought and produced precisely as it was first pitched, anyway. As long as you know the broad outline and arc of your story, the rest of the details, the actual story beats, can be worked out later on.

Even now, you may not get a clear go-ahead. But after everyone in the room has had a chance to mull over the idea some more, and the questions have been asked, you'll most likely get an encouraging nod, and the producer in charge will ask if you've got any other ideas to pitch. I have never been at a pitch session, as either the pitcher or the catcher, where the writer wasn't given at least two shots.

So now you must gather your energies again and trot out your second-best idea, though you do not need to bill it as such. Everyone will know that's how you feel about it, since it wasn't the one that you led off with, but that's okay. I've never had any more, or less, luck with my second, or even third, idea than I had with my first. This isn't a science.

But remember what I said about limiting yourself to a few ideas? When I was story editor at one show, I presided over a particularly uncomfortable session in which a young man who came in to pitch plunked himself down in the chair at the table, then withdrew a quart-sized bottle of Evian water and a three-ring binder filled with papers.

"I've got sixteen ideas to pitch to you today," he declared. "I'll start with the best one, and work my way down."

Sixteen? I didn't know what to say. I thought he was exaggerating.

He threw open the notebook, glanced at the first page, then

launched into his first story idea. In way too much detail, scene by scene, beat by beat.

It was, I'm sorry to say, a mess.

And there are fifteen more? I thought. *Each one worse than the one before it? How could that be?*

He was actually allowed to pitch three or four more ideas before the consensus in the room was clear: The poor fellow did not understand the show or what we we were looking for. I had to gently interrupt him and say that we were, unfortunately, going to have to bring the session to a close. Even though we'd been in there for nearly an hour, he looked stunned at the abrupt conclusion.

"Well, okay," he said uncertainly. "But I've got eleven more ideas to go."

"That's okay," I said. "We really appreciate the work you've put in, but none of these is really going to work for us."

Now he looked positively poleaxed. "What do you mean, none?"

"I mean, we really have very few—"

"Not even the first one, the one about the soldiers?"

"No, I'm sorry—not even the one about the soldiers." I stood up, looking as apologetic as I could, and the guy sat there for another few seconds, glowering. Then he slammed the notebook shut and shoved his almost-empty water bottle into his shoulder bag. One of the other two staff members in the room gave me a look, like, *You want me to call security?*

But the fallen writer elected to depart with no further difficulty. I saw him lingering by the reception desk while his parking pass was validated, then he stalked out in a huff.

Need I even say that he was not called in again, and to the best of my knowledge he has never worked anywhere in TV?

Your own pitch sessions, I know, will go much more smoothly. Even if you come up with sixteen ideas, keep thirteen of them to yourself.

And in even the most unfruitful pitch meeting, where you manage to snare them with nothing, there's *something* you can get out of it. For starters, there's the seasoning. Practice makes perfect and all that. The next time, you'll be better.

If you're able to keep your composure and remain amiable, you may make such a good impression that you'll be invited back, either to pitch again or—if God is smiling upon you—to be given a story idea that the producers themselves have hit upon and started to shape. This isn't so uncommon.

Whatever's happened in the room, from a lovefest to a debacle, your exit from the room is at least as important as your entrance. After you've pitched your three ideas, gather yourself and your things together and thank everyone for their time. If you think you've fallen flat, don't skulk out with your tail between your legs. You might have misread the situation.

If you think you've succeeded, do not try to nail down the sale yourself. It's not your job to negotiate—nor do the producers want to be put on the spot like that. That's for your agent to do. Let him earn his cut.

What should you do if the producers ask if you've got something—say, that one-page précis you were clutching in your hand—that you can leave behind to help them in their deliberations?

Most agents and most writers I know will tell you never, ever, to do that. My friend Lisa thinks it's the worst idea imaginable: "It just gives them something to read over, again and again, until they find things not to like about it. I just want them to remember how much they liked the idea when I first pitched it to them, right there in the room."

And I do know what she's saying. If they liked it while they were hearing it, they should have to pay for the privilege of hearing it again—by offering you a contract for an episode.

What can I say? I'm weak and eager to please. If they ask me for a leave-behind (that's actually what it's called) I almost always oblige. My own feeling is that it might also serve, if a few days pass before a decision is reached, as a good way of reminding them of the virtues the story possessed. Or, if someone who wasn't in the meeting has to be persuaded, I'd rather have my own words (even if it's only a few paragraphs on a single page) do the talking than to rely upon someone else who'd been in the meeting to present the story for me. In a couple of instances, I've actually been present when various producers, acting as my advocate, have pitched ideas of mine to their superiors while I had to sit silent—and let me tell you, it is a harrowing experience. You sit there, politely holding your tongue, while you hear your idea being mangled, torn, and pitched in a way you *know* will never go over. Then, when it does flop, it's of course your fault.

So yes, I do offer the leave-behind, while most writers don't. Don't hate me because I'm spineless.

The Uncertainty Principle

■ ■ ■ One thing I have learned over the years is that you never know for sure when, or if, you've made a sale, until your agent actually gets the call.

I have had meetings where the producers were falling all over me with excitement. With one of them, early on in my so-called career, we had actually gotten as far as sitting on her sofa together, combing through books of head shots, looking for just the right actors and actresses for each of the parts in my script.

That night, I was still so excited I called a friend, who has written for a dozen different shows, and told him how well the meeting had gone and that I'd made the sale! I was beside myself with joy.

"Has she called your agent?" he said, with a surprising lack of enthusiasm.

"No, not yet," I said, "but she loved it! Loved it! And guess who she's thinking of getting to do the guest shot?"

"Has she called your agent?" he repeated dryly.

"No, I told you, we only had the meeting this morning. But she can't wait to get going on it."

"Apparently," he said, "she can."

And now I was starting to get irritated.

"If she hasn't called your agent," he intoned again, "you don't have a deal."

That's when I figured I'd had enough—enough of his negativity, enough of his pessimism. He'd had his share of success, why couldn't he just be happy that I was getting a little piece of my own? What did he have to worry about? He was a millionaire, and I was still pretty much starting out. Was he threatened? By me? By my one little deal?

The call ended badly, and the whole affair with the producer ended worse.

Because my pal, the old pro, was right.

She never did call my agent, and she never took another call from me, either. It was all just blather.

Conversely, you can think you've failed utterly and find out, later, that you've got a deal.

Once, I was pitching to a man who looked for all the world as if he'd fallen asleep in his chair. There were moments when I feared he was going to topple over, he looked so bored. Believe it or not, I started to feel sorry for him, having to sit there and listen to me ramble on and on, in my increasingly hopeless attempt to get an assignment. I just wanted to stop and say, "Haven't we both had enough of this torture? Shouldn't I just call it a day?"

Something told me not to. Something told me to stay the course, which I did. When I did finally leave, he awakened enough to stand up, shake my hand, and even give me a little wave, through the window, as I walked past his office on the way back to my car. I waved back, smiling weakly, already wondering what kind of spin I could put on this disaster when I called my agent to report in.

I don't need to tell you how this story ends. I already have. Within twenty-four hours, *he'd* called my agent (before I'd even worked up the nerve) and had offered me a deal. Thank God I hadn't just thrown in the towel, as I had been so sorely tempted to do. The guy had been awake the whole time, after all.

The moral of the story? Fight the good fight, all the way to the end. You just never know how it'll turn out.

Call-Backs

■ ■ ■ Most of the time when the show's producers have decided that they love your idea and definitely want to do it, you'll be called back in for another conference, only this time it's even more to the point.

Since you are eventually going to have to go off and do an outline, or "beat-sheet" (a brief outline of the action beats, or plot points, in your episode), the producers and writers on staff will want to give you as much direction and input as they can beforehand. Now that you'll indeed be working with them, they will all want to keep you on track as much as possible, partly out of comradely goodwill, and partly because the better you do your job, the easier theirs will be later on.

How this part of the process plays out depends a lot on the show, its staff, where they are in the season (if it's a slow time, they'll be more available to you than if it's a big crunch period), and how quickly you're able to grasp where they want you to go with the script. After one show had decided to pick up an idea of mine, I went in one more time; the producer and his staff lay around on sofas for an hour or two, one of them occasionally stood up and scribbled a few words in Magic Marker on the large greaseboard that hung on the wall, and then it was officially over.

"Got it?" the executive producer said to me as he pulled his car keys out of his pocket.

"I think so," I said, madly trying to decipher and copy down the jottings on the board.

"Great. Go to it."

And that was the only session I had with them before I turned in the outline and got word from the EP's assistant to get started writing the script.

That, I will always remember as the dream trip. Rare, wonderful, and free of creative interference, and it could not have come at a more opportune time, as I had just come off the nightmare voyage that was its perfect, awful counterpart.

On the earlier project, I was writing for a reasonably successful network show (bigger and better known, unfortunately, than the one where things later went so well) but from the get-go I'd run into nothing but trouble.

My first mistake? I had gone to the show-runner, Doug, who was a friend of mine, and I had done what I always swore I would never do—I tainted the friendship by pushing him to give me an episode. At the time, I was not only suffering some serious financial strains, I was also in danger of losing my Writers Guild health insurance, which is contingent upon your landing a certain amount of guild-covered work.

Anyway, those are my excuses for doing what I did, for hammering him, relentlessly, with one idea for the series after another. Every idea was somehow wide of the mark, over the top, not what they wanted to do in the coming season. In all fairness, it was probably as embarrassing for Doug as it was for me—I kept pitching him ideas that didn't fly, and he had to keep shooting them down.

The nadir? That came on the morning Doug decided that he wasn't going to go to the office at all that day—he was going to work from home so that he could watch the World Cup soccer finals on his big-screen TV. He knew that I had some new ideas—more ideas!—so he suggested that I come over to his house and pitch to him there.

Since I'd have gone all the way to Timbuktu in search of a sale, Sherman Oaks wasn't too much to ask. I drove over and found him in his den, glued to the set. You might as well know right now, my interest in professional sports—whether it's soccer, football, basketball, you name it—is about equal to my interest in the mating habits of the dung beetle. Still, I dutifully sat there, trying to get into the spirit of the thing, wondering whether I was supposed to be rooting for Brazil or whoever that other team was, and waiting for the commercial break, during which, I presumed, I would be expected to do a quick pitch.

"Gee," I finally said, "there aren't a lot of commercial breaks, are there?"

Doug, without taking his eyes from the screen, said, "There aren't any."

None? So when, I wondered, was I supposed to do my pitch? As if he'd intuited my thoughts, Doug said, "There's a halftime break. We'll wait for that."

So we lapsed back into silent concentration—man, there was a lot of chasing around after that ball—until the halftime finally came.

But first, Doug had to hit the bathroom, then he had to return a call, then he decided that the den was too public (his wife and one daughter were at home) so we adjourned to the guest bedroom suite, where he had a kind of work-space set up in the back, under the eaves.

And it was there, on a rickety computer chair, that I perched to do my pitch. But even then I didn't have Doug's full attention; for fear that he might miss the start of the second half, he positioned a portable TV behind my shoulder, with the volume turned low, but not off. I tried to recapture his attention, and I thought I'd almost succeeded, when we both heard a muffled laugh from under the bedclothes. And then the blankets visibly shifted.

"Jessica," Doug said, chuckling, "we're trying to have a meeting in here."

"I'm not in here," his daughter called out from under the covers.

I tried to appear amused, but all I could think of was the dwindling duration of the halftime festivities.

"Come on, Jessica, I'm serious," Doug said, though even I could tell this was not a serious tone of voice.

"What'll you give me?"

"How about a trip to Blockbuster, as soon as the game is over?"

"Can I pick out anything I want?"

"Anything that isn't an R."

Maybe soccer fans like to take a siesta, I hoped, *midgame.*

"Deal," Jessica said, popping her mischievous little head out from under the covers.

As she left, Doug again swiveled his chair toward me, but his eyes, I could tell, were resting on the portable TV.

"So, anyway," I resumed, "my idea was that once his sister comes for her visit, she immediately starts to . . ." I trailed off, thinking from the look on Doug's face that something important was happening behind me.

I turned my head toward the TV, where someone with curly black hair was beaming and waving at the crowd.

"That's a famous player, who retired last year," Doug explained, knowing I was not particularly conversant with the sport. "Go on."

I tried to pick up the thread of my story (and a thread is about what it felt like at this point) but it was a hard slog. Gradually, however, I felt myself getting the train back on the tracks, and whether it was due to the overpowering narrative strength of my story, or the fact that the halftime activities had devolved considerably, I felt that I had temporarily recaptured Doug's attention. Enough, in fact, for him actually to look at me, in the reflective glow of the TV screen, and say, "That's a pretty good idea—we've never done anything like that."

They hadn't? It was? Had I finally, after drilling a dozen different dry holes, struck oil?

"What if," he said, "the sister allied herself with the neighbors—we've been wanting to bring them more into the show—and things spiraled out of control from there?"

"Sure, that's a great way to go," I gushed, even though I had no idea how to do it. I'd figure it out later.

"And then," Doug went on, "what if . . ." Suffice it to say, he started at last to focus on the idea, to evince, dare I say it, a growing enthusiasm, which I matched. Now we were getting somewhere. I could sense what he wanted now, and yes, I could think of a way to get there. I suggested something else, which he immediately latched onto.

"Yes, that'd work, definitely," he said.

"And from there, you could do a whole riff where . . ." I was on fire, I was in the groove, my neural synapses blazing away like Gatling guns; Doug was all ears, smiling, attentive, nodding, when suddenly it all ground to a halt.

"The game's on!" he blurted out, leaping from his chair. "Come on!" he said, hurrying toward the den.

He was out of the room before I could even stand up. Nor did I, for several seconds. I just sat there, deflating like a punctured tire. Then I had, much as I'd like to forget it, one of those moments you remember all your life, a moment when you see yourself with unwanted clarity. It was as if I were now hovering, disembodied, on some astral plane and looking down, the way people say they see themselves on the operating table in near-death experiences . . . and what I saw wasn't pretty. A middle-aged white guy, perched pathetically on a broken computer chair, in the back of somebody's dimly lighted bedroom, clutching a scribbled-on legal pad in his lap. The Willy Loman of TV writers, out there on a wing and a smile.

How had it come to this? How did I wind up here? My SATs had been so high.

Nor did the experience measurably improve from there. Even though Doug had initially liked the idea, and did contact my agent to make the deal, he could never really commit to it—not in the sense of ever, finally, signing off on it. What he did instead was keep me coming into the production office, meeting with various staff members, turning in outline after outline, changing one element after another, until the story no longer bore any resemblance whatsoever to the story I had originally pitched. Even the working title changed completely. It had become the Frankenstein of story outlines, stitched together from a thousand different pieces, and lumbering like the monster it was toward a dark and unpromising future.

Pitching to Win

After thirteen story sessions, conducted over a period of a couple of months, I finally got the call from Doug, not to tell me to start writing the actual script at long last, but to tell me, instead, that I could relax. *Relax?*

"There's no rush," he said, "you can write it whenever."

Whenever? Well, from my point of view, there *was* a rush, because if I didn't write and turn in the actual first draft, I would not be owed or entitled to the *money* for the first draft.

"I was planning on writing the script the moment I got the word to go forward," I said.

And that's when he explained that, due to some cast changes and some new ideas for where the series might go, he was reluctantly going to have to step in and write the particular episode I had been working on—the fifth on the season roster—himself. "But we'll just move yours down the schedule a bit."

I heard the death knell ring in my head. Once you start getting bumped, you usually get bumped all the way.

Knowing that, I resolved to plow ahead as fast as I could, before anyone could literally tell me *not* to write the script at all. Until that happened, I might be in the clear, working, I could claim, under the assumption that the script was still being awaited.

For the next six days, I kept my head down, answered the phone only when I had to, ate whatever we had in the cupboard, and completed a script that included every single beat that the staff and Doug had dictated. It might be a monster, yes, but I had it off the slab, walking, talking, and looking, all things considered, not half bad.

I turned it in, called my agent to make sure he knew that I had turned it in, and waited. For days. Weeks. If you must know, I'm still waiting. It was never declared officially dead, never given a proper burial . . . it just lives on, in some weird state of limbo, in that place where scripts that no one wants go. . . . The show wrapped up its shooting schedule last week.

I have sworn never again to ask for such a favor. Never to demean myself, never to discomfit a friend. Doug had never wanted to involve me in the show, and, to be honest, I had sensed that all along but I'd pushed for it anyway, thinking that

I could prove him wrong; I would show him that we could work together, and stay as friendly as ever. Maybe even friendlier, now that we'd have the show in common.

Doug was right and I was wrong, and if there's a lesson to be learned, it's simply this: Take a night job at Kinko's, bus tables at Denny's, sell a kidney, before you unduly importune a friend in the business.

Part V

Script for Success

A Simple Plan

It might be done on a greaseboard, and it might be done on a blackboard.

It might take one session, and it might take ten.

It might be done in the conference room; it might be done in the producer's office.

No matter how it gets done, the first step in writing your script is going to be the production of . . . an outline.

Don't panic. In most instances, you'll create this outline along with the help of one or more staff members on the show. It generally won't have every beat in it, and it may even have some big holes, but it *will* chart the overall arc of the story. The teaser and the act breaks will be driven into the ground like tent pegs, so you can raise the big top around them.

Once this outline is committed to the blackboard, copy it down *verbatim,* and unless you run into some important and unforeseen reason for departing from it, plan on making your first draft hit all of these predetermined marks with a resounding thwack.

Unhappy as you may be to hear this, a solid outline is a TV writer's best friend. Personally, I can't even hear the word *outline* without flashing back to Mrs. Hughes's classroom at Haven Junior High, where we were given news articles or stories and told to break them down into outlines, with a B for every A, a II for every I, indenting properly at every turn. I hated it, not only because I found it boring, but because it made reading—which I generally loved—a chore. Now, instead of absorbing myself in the text, I was constantly stopping to look for things like topic sentences and A's and B's and figuring out how the whole darn thing had been put together. "We murder to dissect," as Wordsworth put it.

Mrs. Hughes was a hard taskmaster, and a good one, and I do have to thank her for that. Despite my best efforts, she taught me the rudiments and importance of outlining, and nowhere does all of that count for more than in TV or screenwriting. When you're writing a script, you have to be aware at all times of structure—the house you're building has to stand on a solid foundation, and you have to put up the walls and windows and chimneys with a constant eye toward the end product. You have to make sure that you follow the blueprint—your outline—very, very carefully, or you'll wind up with a house that doesn't stand.

Make absolutely sure you have the outline *before* you start writing the script.

Ask any TV or screenwriter and he'll tell you the same sad story, about how he'd started writing some script, and was barreling along, inspiration flowing, fingers flying across the keyboard, the words just falling onto the page, the scenes unfolding one after the other . . . until he felt himself slowing down, then faltering, then picking up speed, then stopping altogether, scratching his head, staring at the monitor, wondering how he'd arrived at this particular point and where he was supposed to take the story from here.

Usually, that's where the script ends. The writer not only loses track of his story, he also loses confidence in it, and winds up slipping the twenty or thirty pages, maybe more, into a desk drawer, waiting until the day comes when he feels revved up about it again, or thinks he can approach it with a fresh eye.

Does that day come?

Sometimes. Not often.

Ground zero for this epidemic is always the same—it's the

missing outline. Because the writer could not face the onerous, and daunting, task of composing an outline, of laboriously laying out his plans, of facing up to the problems he'll encounter in plot and character and motivation, he got stuck. Because he didn't want to do the backbreaking and decidedly unglamorous work of figuring out his structure—where the story should properly start, what complications it should juggle in the middle, where it should end—he found himself hopelessly lost in the middle of a dark wood (also sometimes called the second act).

Now, a lot of writers will tell you they're afraid that once they've laid it all out, they'll lose any interest in writing their story, that the joy of discovery is what keeps them motivated, that this lack of a firm game plan allows their characters unfettered freedom . . . but nine times out of ten they're just covering. They hate to do outlines as much as I do, and they'll come up with any reason they can think of to avoid it. Let's face it, while writing is plenty hard, at least it can be fun. Your dialogue can sparkle, the scenes can sizzle, at the end of the day you can look at the mounting stack of pages and feel like you've really accomplished something.

Try that with an outline. "Look, honey, I worked out the plot points in three scenes in a row. Want to see how I did it?"

Believe me, without that outline, the chances that the script will ever make it all the way to completion are very poor indeed. Without an outline, there's the additional danger of creating a bloated monster, a script that bulges with unnecessary scenes and takes all kinds of wacky detours (from some of which there is no return). In TV writing, brevity is not only the soul of wit, it's a fact of life; any scene, any line, any word that doesn't move things forward in one way or another, that doesn't advance the story and strengthen its spine, has got to go. If you feel like getting away with stuff, write a novel. Herman Melville threw in a whole section on cetology. In TV, at the first sign of a cetology section, it's you they'll throw out.

With an outline in hand, every day when you sit down to write, you'll know where you're going. You'll never have to worry about finding yourself bogged down, flailing around, wondering how to get the story moving forward again. You'll already know. On mornings when you're inspired, when the Muse is sitting right there in your lap, you'll just rip along.

On mornings when you're not inspired, when the Muse is clearly still dawdling at a Starbucks somewhere, you'll still be able to get something done; you'll look at the outline and write a few pages. You'll undoubtedly rewrite these later, but you'll have something, however rough, to show for your time when you turn off the computer at the end of the day.

Slow and steady wins the race. Mrs. Hughes taught me that in junior high, too.

Go to Script!

If there are three words that bring unmitigated joy to the heart of a TV writer, those words are: "Go to script."

Once the producer, show-runner, whoever's in charge, tells you to "go to script," it means several things, all of them good.

First, it means you have been released from outline hell. You are not taking any more outline meetings, you are not getting any more outline notes, you can stop trying to *figure out* the story. At this point it appears you've done that to everyone's satisfaction and you can start *writing* it. When I'm told I can go to script, I feel like a horse that's been locked in the stable for weeks, who is finally free to run.

The other reason writers live for those three little words is that they mean money. Once you've been told to go to script, it means you haven't been "cut off at story"—in other words, you and your episode have not been abandoned in the planning stage; you've received the go-ahead to write the first draft, and the first draft payment is the biggest single portion of the script fee.

While I know you're completely uninterested in the financial aspect of TV writing, I think it's worth noting that, with minor variations, the payment for a freelance TV script is broken into three pieces. Just to give you some idea of what those pieces individually amount to, I'm going to break the code of silence and share with you the amounts I received for each stage of a one-hour script I recently completed. (And these fees, by the way, aren't peculiar in any way to me; these are the fees you'd get, too, for writing an episode of that same prime-time, network show.)

The first piece is sometimes called the story payment, or outline money, and in this instance it came to $10,019. (If I'd been paid that much to write those outlines in junior high, I wouldn't have crabbed so much.)

The second piece—the money that was due me once they said "go to script"—was $14,896.80. This is the largest hunk of the fee because, I guess, it is thought to represent the most arduous and time-consuming part of the assignment. (I'd still hand those honors to the outline stage, but that's just me.)

The third, and smallest, portion of the fee is paid for the second (sometimes called the final) draft of the script; this payment came to $1,655.20.

Grand total (before any agency fees or taxes): $26,571.00.

How long have you got before you have to deliver the goods?

Although, again, it depends to some extent on the show, you're generally given about two weeks to complete a first draft of a one-hour drama script or half-hour sitcom. Of course, the first time a producer called to tell me to "go to script" on a one-hour, he gave me only five days to turn it in. This was both a blessing and a curse.

The curse part is easy to explain: to get it done, I had to stay up till all hours, repeatedly slap my face with cold water, and cancel any plans I had to go outside, see friends, have a life.

The blessing, however, was that it didn't give me time to dither and fret (two of my favorite pastimes); I simply had to throw myself into the frigid waters and start swimming for the distant shore. Shivering and exhausted, but exhilarated, too, I made it.

If you've done your homework well—you know the show

cold, your outline is solid—then writing this first draft should be challenging but nothing to fear. The last thing I do, before starting to write the actual script, is read a few pages of one of the show's previous scripts. I find it gets me as deeply into that voice and format as anything is likely to do. Then I put that script aside, take a deep breath, and type "FADE IN."

Now, of course, you already know roughly what the length of your script is supposed to be, where the act breaks should fall, all of that, and it's of course important to keep those things in mind, but it's also important to allow yourself a little room to improvise. Yes, yes, I know, a teleplay is all about structure and brevity and sticking to the point, but sometimes you're going to find the best stuff—the cleverest dialogue, the funniest bits, the most poignant moments—by letting yourself run free a bit. If your first act comes out six pages longer than it should, don't beat yourself up about it. Just be aware of that fact, and remember that once you're done with the whole script, there'll be plenty of time (if you've budgeted your time well) to go back and trim where you have to, add what you've missed, punch up the slow or dull patches.

What's that you say? You won't *have* any dull patches? Then, congratulations—you're only the second writer I've ever known who writes a perfect first draft. (I'm so glad to have company.)

Most writers, poor souls, have to go back and rewrite often. They actually consider it part of their craft.

Two things in that regard. One: If you have some time remaining before your due date, and you've already revised the script as much as you think possible, put the whole thing away in a drawer and try to forget about it for a day or two. (The Roman poet Horace recommended putting your work away for something like nine years before looking at it again with an impartial eye, but in TV the schedules tend to be a bit too tight for that.) You'll be amazed at what can jump out at you after even the shortest time away from it. In one of my own scripts, I only noticed on rereading it several days later that three acts in a row had all begun on separate nights, with no day shots intervening anywhere. The script read like *Long Day's Journey Into Night*, and it was *not* supposed to be that kind of show. But a little quick legerdemain, and I managed to bring some sunlight into the script.

Two: turning a script in to the producers a week (or even several days) before it is due can backfire on you anyway. While you think it makes you look incredibly diligent and proficient, to the producers it can look like you're some kind of show-off. Once, when I submitted something early, it was even suggested to me that if I had taken the extra days remaining before it was due, I'd have ironed out the remaining problems and turned in a stronger script. I swore not to make that same mistake again.

An even bigger mistake is to miss your deadline altogether. When I was on staff, I actually had writers call me more than once and ask "for an extension" (their very words). *An extension?* When I could accomodate them, I did—but ask me if I called those writers with another assignment. I did not. The TV business isn't college, where if your term paper is due, it doesn't really matter to anyone but you and the professor. In TV, deadlines do matter; sets have to be built, locations found, actors hired. The logistics are incredible, and when even one script falls out of its proper spot in the rotation, that can upset all kinds of other schedules down the line.

So have your script done, and ready to go, on time, or perhaps a day before. Print out two hard copies—one for you, one for them—and call the script supervisor in the show's production office. Ask him or her what software program the show uses, then, if you've been using something else, convert your script into the format they can read at the show. As I mentioned earlier, there are half a dozen different script programs used on most of the shows out here, but to the best of my knowledge they can all be converted from one to the other.

In most cases, the show will send a messenger to pick up the disk and the hard copy (the hard copy is just something they can use in a pinch, if the software conversion has created problems). But when a messenger has not been proffered, I have been known to drive the script over myself; it not only gives you the absolute assurance that the script has landed there safe and sound, but it also gives you a chance to say hello to any of the producers you happen to bump into in the hall. It never hurts to help them attach a face to the work, a charming and responsible individual such as yourself, to the brilliantly executed teleplay that has just been turned in right on time.

Taking Notes

After you've submitted a script, there is a brief respite, a small oasis of time, while you wait to hear back from the show.

You can use this time to bite your nails, worry, seal yourself in a darkened room, or you can try to enjoy this temporary release from bondage by going to the movies, reading a good book, having dinner with friends.

I've done both and, trust me, the darkened room routine just increases any paranoid tendencies you might have. Seeing friends is the best idea, especially because once you do hear back from the show, the chances are, you and your script are going to have to crawl back under your rock for a while. There, you will treasure your recent memories of human contact.

How long it takes the show to get back to you is an open question. In one case, I turned in a script on a Friday morning, and that evening the show-runner called to tell me that she thought I'd done a terrific job. "I thought I'd call now," she said, "so you wouldn't have to worry about it over the weekend."

Need I say, that woman is blessed unto the tenth generation?

On other scripts, I've waited indefinitely, but more typically, you'll hear back in four or five days. The Writers Guild rules state that the producers have two weeks to give you their notes, but that's one of those rules that does get bent.

The word *notes*, up until now in your life, has probably been a harmless one. You've had love notes from your sweetie ("I miss you, Oogie-woogums"), notes from your roommates ("I ate your yogurt—please replace"), reminder notes to yourself ("clean up yard before EPA comes back").

But until you've written a TV script, you've never known the terror, the soul-chilling dread, the annihilating fear that this one simple word can convey.

"We've got some notes for you," they'll say when they call. "Can you come in Tuesday morning?"

This is your cue to gird yourself for battle. Summon up every ounce of self-esteem, hammer it into chain mail, and clamp it on under your clothes. Now is the time to look deep into yourself and reaffirm your faith in your own innate worth, your talent, your fundamental sense that you *are* a cherished child of the universe, because what happens in that room come Tuesday morning will not be pretty, and it will not be kind. By the time you're done hearing their notes (that is, their comments, their questions, their corrections to your script) you will question everything from your grasp of grammar to the goodness of corn flakes. You will stagger from the room wondering if Earth still revolves around the Sun, and gravity still holds. You will stare up at the twilight sky and cry aloud, "Is there a God?"

Giving notes is a practice, I have often thought, specifically invented to allow people without a creative bone in their body to pretend they know better than you do how to write. I can't prove that it was created by network executives, but I'd bet on it, heavily.

What happens is, once your script has been turned in, it makes the rounds; sometimes, just one or two writer/producers read it (and that is ideal), but often it makes a grand tour, getting read by everyone from the network execs to the studio guard who stands at the driveway gatepost.

I have had scripts returned to me with written (or scrawled) notes from as many as eleven people on the pages, and of course I don't need to tell you that none of these notes ever agree. While one reader wishes the conflict with the nurse to be brought forward in the story, another one wants it removed completely. While one thinks there are too many laughs per page and not enough drama, another thinks the laughs are way too few and far between. Where one person loves the script and wants an autographed copy, another one hates it so much he's actually paid someone to fumigate his office after reading it.

For the writer, it's like listening at the Tower of Babel.

And yet, it's the writer's job, your job, to make some sense of all this racket and rewrite the script accordingly.

When you come in to get your notes, you'll find one to maybe three people in the room. The longer they spend chatting with you about your weekend and other trivialities, the worse their notes are going to be. They're just postponing the inevitable, trying to soften the blows to come with this shameful pretense of friendship and camaraderie. Not long ago, a producer spent the first twenty minutes with me rattling on about a local election, and by the time he finally ran out of steam I was ready to throw a rope around the rafters and hang myself.

I knew what was coming, and I was right.

Even the worst notes session will begin fairly tamely. There's always *something* nice the producers can find to say about your script, even if it's just your flawless typing. But pretty soon you'll notice their heads dropping down toward the page, and this is your cue to uncap your pen, turn to a fresh page of your legal pad, and brace yourself for the onslaught.

Because here they come . . . your notes.

In most instances, the producers will go through the script page by page, note by note, asking each other, "Have you got anything to add to that?" If everyone agrees that they have covered all the problems present on that page, they'll move on.

If not, they'll confer, debate the issue among themselves (often as if you weren't even there), and then come, one hopes, to a unanimous decision.

It's your job to sit there like some medieval amanuensis, keeping track of the debate, jotting down their notes, recording their final verdicts. Once in a while you may actually be asked for your opinion, not that it counts for much, or given the chance to explain yourself, as in "What were you going for here?" The fact that they have to ask the question at all means that *whatever* you were going for, you obviously didn't get there in their view. One thing I've learned is not to argue the point; if they didn't get it, they didn't get it. Move on.

By the time you've reached the end of your script, you'll have a legal pad covered with notes, questions, inconsistencies (in the producers' view) that have to be resolved. Often, the main guy will give you back his copy of your script, with his annotations all over it. "If you have any questions or problems while you're doing the next draft," he'll say, "don't hesitate to call."

At this precise moment, that guy is the last person in the world you would ever willingly talk to again, but smile your most gracious smile, thank everyone for their insightful commentary, and take your leave.

On the way home, you might want to stop and pick up a fifth of Wild Turkey, because there is one more blow that is yet to fall—and that comes when you actually read through the notes scrawled on that producer's copy of your first draft.

Let me back up for a moment, to say that I came to the world of TV writing from the much quieter, more genteel precincts of New York book publishing. There, you would have six months, a year, two years if you needed it, to finish a project, and during that time it was quite possible to hear nothing (maybe a card at Christmas, but no more) from your publisher.

When you did eventually finish and turn the manuscript in, you were taken to a lavish lunch at a nice French restaurant, where somewhere over coffee and profiteroles, the editor would gently introduce the topic of changes. At one such lunch, I remember the editor signing the back of the bill (her publishing house had an open account there) before finally saying, "As for the book . . ."

By that point, I'd assumed that she hadn't read it yet, and that this lunch was just a way of celebrating my having turned it in. "Yes?"

"I do have some suggestions."

"Oh," I said, "you've read it, then?"

"Of course I have—didn't you know that? And it's wonderful, just wonderful—so full of life and vitality."

My defenses shot up like a porcupine's quills.

"But I was wondering," she said, "and this is, of course, entirely up to you, you're the author and I don't mean in any way to usurp your creative prerogatives, but it did seem to me that the book might just be tighter, in the sense of being more integrated and powerful, though not necessarily shorter, if the protagonist were to encounter his nemesis, Lord Sykes, just a few chapters sooner in the book?"

She let the endless question hang there in the air, while she waited, fearfully, for some sort of authorial explosion, which, given my docile nature, never came. Besides, she did have a good point; it was a change I'd even thought of making myself, before turning the book in, but sheer lassitude had kept me from getting around to it.

"Hmm," I said, not wanting to give the game away. "That's interesting."

Relieved and encouraged, she smiled, and proceeded then to suggest (always *suggest*, never demand) a few more, very minor alterations to the 420-page manuscript. And when we parted company a few minutes later, under the awning of the restaurant, I went home, thought long and hard about her suggestions, made the ones that were really easy to do, decided *on artistic grounds alone* not to do the ones that were too hard (such as moving Lord Sykes forward in the story), and sent in the changes two weeks later.

We never again spoke of that lunchtime conference, or of the changes I had neglected to make, and even when the book tanked and sold eleven copies, the editor never threw it in my face.

• • •

Anyway, I tell you all this so you will fully understand the shock I felt when I actually had a chance—no, the unavoidable obligation—to read my first set of script notes.

The pages of the script looked like a classroom of third graders had used them for scratch paper: There were markings, arrows, circles, and barely decipherable words, or their cryptic abbreviations, splattered all over the margins, the spaces between the lines, scratched in some cases on the back of the page. "Stilted!" "CUT THIS!" "Shoe leather!" "Weak!" "NO!" "Yuck!" "Awk" (for *awkward*). "OTT!" (for *over the top*). "Ugh" (for *ugh*). It sounded like all those BAMS! and OOFS! and ARGHS! you see in comic book balloons.

Where was the sensitivity? Where was the decorum? Were they unaware that they were dealing with an *artiste*?

There wasn't a page unscathed. In some instances there was just a brutal slash of red ink through whole speeches, in others there was a written comment or correction. Around a mention of the River Thames, a producer, offended for some reason, had made a big wide circle and written "No more Ireland!"

Just for good measure, I thought, *I'll take out England, too.*

I was reeling, appalled, watching as my hoped-for career in TV unwound before my eyes. They hated me! I was useless! Untalented! A worthless blot on the escutcheon of the show! Why had they even allowed me to live?

They shouldn't have.

I would take my own life.

It was the least I could do.

This sort of thinking went on for about a half hour. Then the sedatives kicked in, and I became calm enough to read the notes over with a little more distance, objectivity, reason.

Okay, I thought as I went over each one, I can change that. I can tone that down. I can cut that. I can make that clearer. Sometimes I even saw what the producer was getting at; sometimes, quite frankly, I did not.

But my job, I knew, was not to question why. It was simply to make the changes requested, as well as I could make them, and return the revised script to their offices.

What I did not know then, but learned as I wrote for other

shows and got other sets of notes back on my scripts, was that none of this was all that unusual. True, this particular set of notes, from this particular show, was less civil than most, but brutal candor and harsh brevity was to some extent the order of the day. The politesse of New York publishing was not to be expected in the cutthroat world of network TV. If your feelings got hurt easily, you were going to be in pain a lot of the time.

It's not personal—it's just business.

Or at least that's the line you get.

Not that I've ever entirely bought it.

I have my own theories for what I consider the needlessly callous tone of the notes you get. Chiefly, it's that TV writers have received so many unkind notes themselves that, like grown-ups who beat their kids because they were beaten themselves, they lash out at other writers in turn. It's just the way they were brought up.

A corollary to that is that many TV writers are angry, bitter, frustrated creatures. Don't ask me why—that's a whole 'nother kettle of fish. But in much of this business, a kind of macho attitude prevails; it's a competitive, aggressive culture that says, "If you can't stand the heat, go get a job teaching social studies." And that attitude comes out in the tenor and content of the notes you're given.

Of course, if taken to task for it, these same writer/producers would say, as one of them did when I brought it up to him, "I haven't got time to coddle writers. There's a lot of pressure in this job, and I can't be worrying about hurt feelings—and frankly, we pay well enough that anybody who needs it can go out and get all the therapy they need."

I might have bought into this, or at least acknowledged that it *might* be true, had I not assumed my own staff job, as a story editor, a year later. I too had to read a lot of scripts, and give notes, and guess what? I found it was no more difficult, and no more time-consuming, to give gentle, respectful, even jocular notes than it was to ruthlessly download my own frustrations or weariness onto the writer. I'm no saint, but I saw no reason that I had to be a schmuck. What would be the point?

And though I wish I could say the network types and nonwriting executives were guilty of worse crimes in this department than my fellow writers, it's just not so. Some of the most insulting and demeaning notes I've ever read came to me from other writers, or were written on scripts (which I happened to see) that were on their way back to other freelancers. I often think if this is all the respect writers can muster for each other, then it's no wonder the rest of the industry treats us with such contempt.

For the time being, just remember it's a quirk of the trade. If you get a set of hostile, rancorous notes, do not panic. It's not you, and it's probably not your work. Cold comfort though it may be, you can look at them as an affirmation of your status. You're being treated as rudely and shabbily as a pro.

Most of the time you've got about a week, give or take, to make the changes to your script and turn in the second draft.

And now, here's the good news.

After that, you're done.

Once you've made the requested changes to the best of your ability (or even not), you're through. You have fulfilled your obligations, as stipulated by the Writers Guild of America contract, and you are not only done, you cannot be required to make any further changes.

Not that that means you won't be *asked*. Cajoled. Encouraged. Not that the producer might not try to characterize your second draft—which was all you were required to deliver—as something else instead; he'll call it "a polish" or a "revised first draft."

Just don't fall for any of it—it's all blarney. Producers are famous for playing upon writers' insecurity, their neediness, their fears. They may imply that they'll put the word out on the Hollywood grapevine that the writer is "difficult" and "hard to work with." They'll suggest that if you don't keep quiet and play ball, you'll "never work in this town again."

It's all nonsense, and asking for extra work, with no extra pay, is a violation of the guild contract. If it truly becomes a problem, have your agent make a call for you. If he won't do it, trust me, the guild will be only too happy to do so.

■ ■ ■ **Part VI**

Career Moves

Laws, Sausages, and Scripts

■ ■ ■ Like an unwed mother who gives up her child for adoption, once you've turned in your script you're better off if you don't know where it's gone or what's happening to it now.

The news might be wonderful (maybe it's been adopted by George Lucas, who's turning it into a weekly series), but it also might not be (a team of hacks are tearing it limb from limb).

Suffice it to say, the script is now out of your hands, and it has entered the processing plant, where it will be turned into a typical episode of the show. There's an old saying, No one should ever watch laws or sausages being made. The same might be said of TV shows.

The writing and producing staff of the show will take your script and make all kinds of changes, even a total overhaul. You will not be advised, consulted, or notified. Awhile back, I found myself on the set of *Murder, She Wrote*, and I picked up a copy of the shooting script, which listed all of the drafts on the front cover. If I tell you there were something like fifteen drafts listed there, I would not be kidding, and they were still tinkering with it on the set.

The best thing you can do is put it out of your mind. Go on to your next project, your next proposal, your next spec. Stay focused on what comes next in your career.

If you, or your agent, think there's a chance of your getting another episode of this same show, by all means pursue it. Assuming this first script went well, the producers may well be disposed to give you another, but through no fault of your own, they also may not be so disposed. The freelance opportunities on any show are few and far between, and there's a lot of writers to whom the staff may want to parcel one out. Getting one script assignment is a coup; getting two is a miracle.

At some point down the line, maybe a month later, you will receive what's known as a Notice of Tentative Writing Credit (NTWC), or Credits Proposal, and on it you'll see listed all the other writers on staff at the show, their respective agents (always interesting information), and most importantly how your credit, at the beginning of the televised show, is going to read.

WRITTEN BY <u>YOUR NAME HERE</u>.

If it says anything other than that (let's say, it's a shared credit and you don't see any reason why that should be) then you have until the date on the bottom of the notice (usually five to ten days later) to file a protest with the Writers Guild and with the credits administrator whose whereabouts are also indicated on the notice. Then, if the question isn't somehow easily and amicably settled, it will go to an arbitration proceeding, conducted by the guild. (More about that under "Taking Credit," beginning on page 211.)

While seeing your name on that credits notification is a definite thrill, it's nothing, of course, compared to seeing it on your TV screen, and that is one of the glories of TV.

You can write a book and wait two or three years just to see a single copy land on the bottom shelf of your neighborhood bookstore. But in television, what you write today can be translated to film tomorrow, and a month later you can see it listed in your weekly *TV Guide*. It's not exactly instant gratification, but it's awfully close.

Nor is this the time for modesty. You should alert all your friends and family to the date, the channel, the hour (in their time zone) that your creation will premier onscreen. People need advance notice if they're going to have to learn how to set their VCR.

Just don't forget to warn them of one thing: If they want to see your credit (and why else would they be tuning in?) they are going to have to sit tight. As you well know, there's an endless scroll of writers, producers, and actors at the beginning of any TV episode, but the teleplay credit—yours—is the next to last (just before the director) to appear on the screen. My mother always gives up hope too soon and leaves the room to go and get something before my credit finally shows up. To this day, I believe she thinks I'm lying about what I do.

But this is the part that makes it all worthwhile—you're sitting on your sofa, watching your name appear on the screen, seeing your story (however altered) told, hearing actors and actresses utter your lines, on costly sets built to accommodate your imaginings. You've created something, something that would not have been made without you (that *could* not have been made without you), and your work, your words, are entertaining millions of people, all over the country.

It's a heady sensation, hard-won and well-deserved, so sit back and enjoy it.

United We Stand

■ ■ ■ You are also one precious step closer to the Holy Grail of every writer in Hollywood—health insurance—more specifically, the health insurance that comes with membership in the Writers Guild of America.

Sure, the WGA protects your artistic privileges, guarantees generous fees for your services, collects piles of residuals from every signatory studio, production company, and network, monitors your earnings from all parts of the globe, speaks on your behalf in defense of your commercial and creative rights, throws swell shindigs at its headquarters office . . . but what writers really prize is its health insurance policy. It's so good, you can't wait to get sick.

The health coverage pays most or all of your medical bills, from doctor visits to teeth cleanings, from eyeglasses to prescription drugs. Once a year, you can even rack up a full physical, just for the fun of it.

The best way to acquire this miraculous coverage is to write scripts for guild-signatory companies, and at the same time start accumulating the credits that will eventually earn you full membership in the guild. To qualify for that honor, you have to earn a certain number of units (twenty-four, to be exact)—and unless you've written and sold a full-feature screenplay or you've just been signed to a thirteen-week TV staff contract or some equally marvelous deal has just landed in your lap, the chances are, you haven't yet qualified.

Even after you've been hired to write your first thirty-minute sitcom or one-hour teleplay, what you've taken is only the first step toward clearing the bar. Depending on the extent of the guaranteed work that you've been commissioned to do, you've earned a certain number of units, and once the signatory company notifies the guild of your employment, you'll receive an application for associate membership, which will run you seventy-five dollars per year, and grant you an assortment of minor privileges, like getting to join the Film Society or the Inter-Guild Credit Union.

With your next assignment, or the one right after that, you are probably going to be expected, perhaps even required, to join the guild. (Not that anyone in his right mind would resist the invitation.) It's a curious situation, really—you must *earn* the right to enter the golden portals of the guild, but once you've earned that right, you don't really have a *choice* about exercising it. If you've acquired twenty-four units' worth of work with signatory companies, and you plan to work again in this town, you *must* join. Think of it, in the immortal words of Don Corleone, as an offer you can't refuse.

This membership arrangement is perhaps the reason the guild has managed to remain as strong as it has. Early on, writers in Hollywood got together and agreed on a few things, like how much they were going to get paid. (Go ahead, ask me how fervently I wish that novelists, or journalists, had been able to do the same thing.) By sticking together, the TV and screenwriters were able to demand, and get, most of the working conditions, rights, and, above all, monies, to which they were entitled—and this from an industry bound and determined to give nothing away. If today you think TV and screenwriters are the best-paid and best-protected group of writers in the galaxy, you'd be right, but that isn't to say the battle is ever over. With every renegotiation, the studios and networks try to chisel away at the WGA's Minimum Basic Agreement (the MBA), and the guild has to wave the club of an industrywide strike. Sometimes, the club has to fall, and strikes happen. Only then does the rest of the industry fully awaken to the fact that it really does all start with the written word.

When your time comes to join the Writers Guild, you'll have to swallow hard for just one moment—the initiation fee is a fairly steep $2,500. After that, you have to pay quarterly dues of twenty-five dollars, plus 1½ percent of your earnings.

While the guild can do a lot for you, from pursuing your residuals to making sure that your employers abide by the terms of the MBA, there are also a few things it *can't* do.

Most notably, the guild can't do a thing about finding you work. It's not an employment agency. In fact, in any given year, about half of the eight thousand members of the guild (and that's the total, in the Writers Guilds East and West) don't find any work at all. In case you weren't aware already, writing for the screen is a highly paid, but very precarious, profession.

Nor can the guild pull your feet out of the fire if you become entangled, against guild rules, with a nonsignatory company. Doing so is not only a good way to get professionally manhandled, it's also a great way to wind up getting fined, or worse, by the guild—which doesn't look kindly on such transgressions.

"You mean, if somebody who's not a signatory wants me to write something, and I'm a member of the guild, I have to say no?" you may ask.

Yes, my friend, you do have to decline, and believe me, it's a blessing in disguise. Just last week I was opportuned yet again by an old friend of my mother's who was dying to have me write a treatment of her life—"I started the first sorority at my college, and the stories I could tell!"—and she was more than willing to pay me for my troubles. "Such a movie this would make! That Jenna Elfman, the one from the *Dharma* show, she could play me! She's the spitting image of me at that age."

But like Van Helsing warding off Dracula with a cross, I was able to hold up the guild agreement and say, "Much as I would love to write it—'cause I'm sure it's a great story—I *can't*! I'm a member of the Writers Guild."

"So I'll pay you."

"That makes no difference—you're not a signatory to the contract. And I can't work outside of it."

"So I'll pay you under the table."

"If the guild were to find out, I'd be in big trouble."

"Who's going to tell them?"

She had me there, for a second. Then I said, "The minute we tried to take your story to Steven Spielberg, or Oliver Stone, or Brian de Palma—the obvious candidates—the truth would come out."

Now she was stymied, because she sure as shootin' didn't want to pay for a treatment or a script that she couldn't show to Steven Spielberg—that was the whole *point*—without starting some kind of a ruckus.

"What I *can* do," I said, "is suggest a very fine writer who's not yet a member of the guild."

"Why isn't he? He's no good?"

"No, he's just new in town. He used to be a professor." That, I knew, would intrigue her.

"Professor?" she said, taking the bait. "Where?"

"Amherst."

And that sealed the deal. I was able to use the guild-member defense to get out of doing a project I had no interest in doing all along, and at the same time my friend from Amherst was able to make some money writing a treatment for the "Sorority" story. (Not only that, he actually liked the idea, which did give me a terrible moment's pause. Had I just passed on a blockbuster concept?)

There is, for the record, one more way to get into the WGA, a less expensive way, and it's the route I happened to take myself, although I didn't know it at the time.

My first big writing job was on a show that was shot up in Canada (an increasingly common phenomenon, you will discover) and as a result I had to join the Writers Guild of Canada.

Career Moves

I don't remember exactly, and the figure has undoubtedly changed since then, but after factoring in the Canadian exchange rate and all that, I think my membership in the WGC cost me no more than a couple of hundred dollars, and the cut the Canadian guild took out of my paycheck was also lower.

Even better, when I later started writing for a show shot right here in the States, and it became compulsory for me to join the American guild, I learned that the two guilds had a reciprocal agreement; in other words, the much larger American initiation fee was waived for members in good standing of the Canadian guild.

So if, by chance, your talents should be enlisted on a Canadian production *before* an American one, do not hesitate to join the Writers Guild of our welcoming cousins to the North. They're a very friendly lot, with a funny way of talking, great beer . . . and hard-to-beat entry fees for writers.

The Great Divide

Among TV writers, there is a huge gulf that separates the truly blessed from the struggling multitudes.

On one shore, where the ground is sere and the trees barren, you have thousands of freelance writers, scrambling to get pitch meetings, script assignments, parking passes.

On the other, where the lawns are emerald green and the trees in blossom, you have the writers who have managed to land not just an assignment, but a . . . *staff job*. The brass ring. The pot of gold at the end of the rainbow. The most coveted prize in TV.

When you're on staff, you have a contract, which guarantees you a certain number of weeks, or months, of work, and the salary is generous.

You have an office, with your very own computer—probably a later and better model than the one you use at home.

You might even have an assistant. (I used to have to share mine, but that was okay. The most important thing I ever had him do was install the antiquated Word Perfect 5.1 in my laptop.)

You have a parking space, perhaps assigned to you alone.

You have a title, generally one that sounds impressive to anyone who doesn't know better.

You have a place to go when you get up in the morning, and a place to bitch about when you get back home (sometimes many, many hours later).

Best of all for a writer, better even than the regular income, better than the credit, the title, the secretary, is this: When people ask you what you do, you don't have to bumble around, mentioning this or that spec script you've finished, or the option deal that expires next week, or the novel you've started for the sixteenth time. You can look 'em in the eye and say, "I'm a writer for *Law and Order*."

That shuts 'em up fast.

How do you get there? How do you land one of these lucrative and much-sought-after staff jobs?

If there were a road map, it would sell for a fortune. But there isn't. So the best way to secure a staff job is the plodding, old-fashioned way: Write the best scripts you can, and then hope for the best.

Over time, you will accumulate, slowly but surely, more and more scripts, some of them produced, some of them just specs, but all of them examples of your range and versatility.

You're also going to accumulate contacts—people you have worked with, who know you now, who liked you and your work. Do you remember, for instance, that show you sold your first episode to? (As if you could ever forget.) Where did all those producers and staff writers go since then? Have some of them moved on to other shows, where they might now be in a position to pull you on board?

It's those two things (the scripts you've written and the people you now know) that will help you make your way in the TV business. You have the two essentials for landing a staff job—now you just need (and never dismiss this) a little bit of luck. The "right place at the right time" formula works as powerfully in TV as in anything else—maybe more so. But luck, as we all know, favors the well-prepared.

And please, don't pay too much attention to the naysayers, who are legion in this town. I have one very dear friend who never tires of reciting, "Staff jobs are im-poss-i-ble to get. They are im-poss-i-ble to get." He dismisses the whole notion with a shake of his head. "Don't even think about it. It's im-poss—"

I know, I know. And he does have a point; staff jobs are hard to land. Everyone wants them, and a large part of getting one is knowing the right people, who will bring you in and give you serious consideration for the post.

But please . . . *impossible*?

I don't think so.

Just look at the number of shows on the air, look at the endless list of writers and producers that unscroll at the top of each one, look at all the different channels, and all the different shows that those channels run, and remember (not that you would ever forget) that every one of those shows, every episode, has been written by somebody, somewhere.

TV at times may look to an outsider, as it long did to me, like a huge, unconquerable kingdom, but it is in fact a patchwork made up of a thousand different fiefdoms, and every one of those fiefdoms needs willing hands to toil in its fields. As long as you're willing to get your hands dirty, someone, eventually, will hand you a hoe.

End of sermon. Better yet, end of labored metaphor.

Stalwarts and Pilots

■■■ Given the turmoil in the TV business, shows faltering right out of the gate, the networks eroding, the cable channels proliferating, it's now possible for a writer to land a staff job at virtually any time of the year.

Still, the chances are better during what's commonly known as staffing season, which runs from March to June, roughly. The more established shows, the ones that know they're coming back, start hiring earlier, and the others concentrate their efforts in late April, May, and June. That's when the networks look over their schedules and try to decide what to drop, what to move, what new shows to plug in and where to put them.

The network honchos preserve, of course, the out-and-out hits—the *E.R.*s and *X-Files*s and *Drew Carey*s. That's the easy part of their job. They also drop the absolute duds. That's even easier.

Then there are the shows that are, as they say in the business, "on the bubble." Their ratings aren't so bad that they should be summarily canceled, but they aren't so good that they should automatically be renewed. Will their ratings improve with another season on the air, or will they plummet further? Have they tapped their maximum audience, or are there millions of people out there who simply have yet to find these shows? The network execs, in all their putative wisdom, must make the call.

Finally, there are the pilots—the initial scripts for the new shows that the various networks hope to launch. These have originated all over, from lone writers sitting in rented rooms, comedy teams in development deals, production companies, feature screenwriters, and they come in all shapes and sizes.

These pilots also come in every degree of quality from dismal to superb. I have read many that were so mind-numbingly dumb and insensitive, you can hardly believe the writers were paid by anyone (and they *were* paid by *someone*) to write them. Even now, a few of these disasters, which, thank God, died swiftly and largely unnoticed, spring to mind:

The action/adventure that starred a macho black detective who, after each arrest, liked to declare "Afri-*can*!"

Or the show set in a dark, dysfunctional city of the future, run by ruthless gangs of beautiful babes.

Or the one where six-foot-tall talking termites took their deadly revenge on mankind.

At the same time, I have read pilot scripts that made immediate sense, scripts where you could *see* the show in your mind's eye right off the bat. With these, all you had to do was read the first episode and you knew immediately who the characters were, what the show was about, and, most importantly, where it was likely to go each week.

That last qualification is, in some ways, the trickiest—where *is* the show going to go each week? While it's hard enough to write a sitcom or one-hour drama in which the characters are likable and interesting, and the whole story holds together, what's even harder is figuring out a setup, a premise, a template if you will, which will allow for future stories. The brilliance of *The X-Files*, for example, lies chiefly in its simplicity: every week, FBI agents Mulder and Scully embark on a different case. That's their job—it's even the title of the show.

The hospital dramas and the cop shows revolve around a core of characters, who work in a dynamic setting where story opportunities are literally wheeled in on stretchers each week, or collared on the street. That's one reason there are so many of these shows—the stories have high stakes and a built-in urgency. It's also why you see so few dramas about accountants and file clerks.

The sitcoms rely even more heavily than the dramas upon character, since their stories are generally flyweight at best—you've just got to like and care about the host of "Tool Time," or how Will and Grace are getting along, or whether Jamie and Paul will remain mad about each other. Audiences tune in to see Dharma astound, bewilder, and enchant Greg each week.

What kills more pilots than almost anything else is this strange lack of foresight, this inability from the creators themselves, to look down the line and ask, "What happens in the third episode of the series? Or the thirteenth?" I have one friend, a very smart and successful TV writer/producer, who wrote a pilot script that was so epic in its intentions and so confused in its execution, that all I could do, after reading it, was say, "Wow. That's a pretty amazing piece of work."

"It is, isn't it?" he said, glowing.

"But I'm wondering where you're planning to go with it."

"NBC, first."

"No, I meant, Where is the show going to go? Now that your heroine is stranded inside this video game, what happens to her?" Then I asked the fatal question. "What will happen in, say, the third episode?"

My friend glowed even more brightly. "I don't know." He said it with all the gravity you would use to explain that you had just cracked forever the subatomic code.

"Is that what you're going to tell NBC, if they ask?"

"Yes."

"Well, okay, maybe that's what you'll tell *them*," I said, stalling. "But of course *you* know where it's all going, right?"

"That's what's so great about it," he said, smiling like the Cheshire cat. "I don't know."

Now, given my friend's illustrious credentials, and the appallingly obtuse nature of most network execs, that explanation actually worked for a while. The first meeting or two, according to my friend, went very well, and every time he uttered his portentous "I don't know," a profound shudder went through the room. The creative execs felt themselves in the presence of greatness, blinking as it were at the dawn of a new creation. *My God*, they were thinking, *maybe what we've just heard is the next . . . Twin Peaks."*

My friend was carried along on a wave of giddy exuberance for several weeks—here was a project, the execs believed, that had class written all over it!—until, as I expected, the whole mess finally hit the wall. At some point, the pilot had fallen into the hands of a more senior exec, one who actually had it in her power to "greenlight" (that is, actually commit to make) projects. When she asked that uncomfortable question, "What happens in the third episode?" and my friend intoned his cryptic "I don't know," it failed to work its magic.

"I don't either," she said, dismissing the project.

Don't lose any sleep over this tale—my friend had such a long track record that he quickly landed a job on another, pre-existing show, where a fierce but loving family resolves a personal crisis each week.

As it happens, I've just come across the list of last year's pilot pickups, sent to me at the time by my agent, and I decided to conduct a little experiment. The list is eight pages long, and it includes 142 new shows, both sitcoms and dramas. Reading over it now, I see that out of the 142, only seventeen are actually still on the air, and most of those are just barely hanging on. I'd say six, if they're lucky, will make the next cut. The odds, as you can see, of a new show getting launched, much less succeeding, are not good.

But for the purposes of staff employment, especially for newcomers, these pilots are as good a bet as any. Unlike the older shows, which are simply up for renewal, and which already have a complement of established, entrenched writers, these new shows have to hire a staff from the ground up. The creator and the show-runner are already on board, but now they've got to fill all the other slots, the ones lower down the totem pole, and yours is just the kind of head that would fit neatly on a lower portion of the pole.

It's your agent's job to make sure your head gets considered. To do that, he first has to make sure you have the opportunity to see, and read, as many of these pilots as possible. He should be dumping a wheelbarrowful of pilots on your doorstep. He should also give you his best assessment of which ones are going to fly, and which ones are going to die aborning. This is the kind of insider info agents are supposed to possess and offer to their clients.

In addition, a good agent should also provide a few helpful connections to some of these shows—other clients, for instance, who are already on board.

Then, it's up to you to do some culling of your own. You have to decide which of these shows you think you'd like to write for, which ones you find funny or moving, and which ones you feel have some potential as a series (can *you* figure out what the third episode would be?). Ask your agent to get you a meeting with the producing team. After all, what's the point of having developed such fantastic pitching powers if you're never going to wind up and throw?

The Back Door

■ ■ ■ Everything I've said so far about getting on staff at a show is pretty reasonable and logical; I'm not going to recant any of it now, but I am going to add this caveat: Many of the people I know who are now happily ensconced on staff at one show or another found their way there by some much more circuitous route.

One was a journalist who was assigned a magazine piece about a certain show, interviewed the producers there, and wound up getting a job.

One was a comedienne who had a brother—yes, nepotism rears its familiar head—who was a cameraman on a show. She went to visit him on the set and fell into an animated conversation with one of the producers, who invited her to submit some ideas, and before you know it she was working on staff.

One was an off-Broadway playwright who had a literary agent who moved out West, became a development exec, then turned around and hired the playwright to write for one of the shows he was developing.

The one thing that all of these people had in common was that they *wrote*, whether it was magazine articles, comedy sketches, or one-act plays. They were authors, comics, playwrights, reporters (*a lot* of TV staff writers have come from the ranks of journalism) but whatever it was, when it came to writing for TV, they were able to call upon the same professional attitude and disciplined habits that they'd used in their previous work.

The fact that they were writers, even if up until that time they'd never so much as *seen* a script, is also how they caught the attention of someone in the TV industry.

So while you're waiting for the call-back from the studio, or praying that the agent will like your spec script enough to send it out, or combing through the pilots for the upcoming season, write.

If it's not a spec script, make it an essay for the newspaper's op-ed page; make it a book proposal; make it a short story aimed at the literary journals; or a blockbuster novel aimed at the best-seller lists.

Make it anything at all, just so long as it keeps your writing muscles limber and strong; if it also manages to make some public impression—when it's printed in the newspaper, performed on a tiny nightclub stage, included in a short story collection—that's even better, much better, because you absolutely never know who will read it, who will attend the performance, or who will see in it something that piques their interest in the work. Or in you, the author of it.

If I sound a little like I'm promoting the unconventional route, maybe I am—because I am a prime example of how it can work.

To be completely honest with you, I never really planned on getting into TV writing at all.

Did I think I was too good for it?

Not at all.

Did I think I wasn't good enough?

Not at all.

But when I came to L.A., the whole TV business looked so foreign, so forbidding, to me, that I never really thought I could make a dent in it. The walls seemed so high and impenetrable, I didn't even know where to bang my head against them. Anytime that I did evince even the slightest interest in writing for

TV, there was someone (a friend, an agent, a know-it-all) ready to tell me how difficult it was, and how, for someone like me, *at my age*, out of the question.

At my age? True, I was no longer in my twenties (hell, I was seriously into my thirties by then) but I hadn't really been thinking of myself as over the hill quite yet. In New York, I was still considered young—my editors, my publishers, my agent, they were all older than I was. And for a man *my age*, I still looked okay. (I was one of those guys that people always said would look better as he got older. So far, there's no evidence of that, but I still hold out hope for my nineties.) But I've got my hair (or most of it), my teeth are still my own, my posture's as good as it ever was. On a New York subway, I looked to be in better shape than most of the other passengers.

Of course, the minute I got to L.A., I knew I was going to be held to a higher standard. What passes in New York does not pass here.

Here, people really do work out; it's not enough just to be thin, you have to be toned.

Your hair has to be more than cut and combed; it's supposed to have body, and sheen.

Your skin has to look vital and sleek; the ashen pallor I had worn so well in Manhattan looked just plain cadaverous in the California sun.

All of the things I could change, I did—sort of. I got out more, picked up a little color, lost a few pounds, found a great barber who, as long as you could stand his New Age nattering, did wonders with my lackluster coif. I did draw the line at exercising.

And as for my age, there was nothing, other than lying, that I could do about that, but concealing my true age seemed just too darn depressing, and I have never understood the logic of it. I'd rather have people know the truth, and think, "Gee, for thirty-eight he doesn't look so bad," rather than lie about it, and have them think, "He's thirty-one? Whew, I guess that's what disappointment in life can do to you." To me, it always made more sense to lie *upward*. Tell people that you're ten years older than you are, so they're blown away by how *good* you look for your age.

But in L.A., and in the TV business in particular, youth rules. As one friend put it, when I mentioned that I'd like to get into TV, "You've got a better chance of becoming an astronaut."

Never one to find hope where others have already told me there is none, I put TV on the back burner. Yes, I'd written that spec script, and I'd bugged my agent once or twice, but I had pretty much written off TV as a viable option, and instead I was working, now and again, on feature film scripts.

For movies, I figured, no one would care if I was fast closing in on forty. If they found out, they could just buy the script, dump me, and hire some high school kid to do the rewrites.

But you know how they say you always find true love the moment you stop looking for it? In a way, that's what happened to me.

I was back to writing books, and doing it fairly happily. The last one had been a nonfiction study of black magic and the occult, entitled *Fallen Angels*. The book was my response to the whole angel craze that I'd smacked straight into when I came to L.A.

At that point, angels were everywhere, in bookstores, on calendars, greeting cards, you name it. People out here, including, of course, my barber, believed that there were angels watching over us all the time, protecting us against everything from tax audits to bad hair days. And frankly, it was driving me crazy. If people were going to believe in good angels, I thought, then they might as well believe in the bad ones, too, and I'll write the book about 'em.

When I called my New York literary agent, a woman known as much for her withering intelligence as for her brutal candor, and told her about the angel fad and my idea to counteract it, she said, "Robert, that's just L.A. I warned you not to go there."

But I knew this wasn't just a Los Angeles phenomenon. True, you can count on L.A. to embrace inanity with an ardor unseen in more sensible spots (one of my friends actually thinks he was an alien abductee, and the *Los Angeles Times* runs a regular column on how to design your home in keeping with the pseudo-scientific principles of *feng shui*), but I felt in my bones that this angel stuff was going to go nationwide. For once, I was right.

The book I wrote on the bad angels came out just in time to catch the backlash, and it did very well, both here and abroad, with translation rights to five countries.

And so, the stage was set for what happened next.

I was sitting at a card table at the Midnight Special bookstore, behind a stack of copies of *Fallen Angels*, when a tall guy with a moustache and a bookbag slung over one shoulder loitered at my table. He picked up a copy, thumbed through it, put it down.

I was used to this. To make a sale, you have to engage the customer in a subtle dance, you have to capture his attention in some casual, oblique, disinterested manner. "Please buy the book," I said. "I'll never ask you for anything else again as long as I live."

"I guess you're the author," he said.

Was it so obvious?

Anyway, we started talking, and Bill turned out to be a screenwriter who'd written a bunch of horror and sci-fi pictures. After a few minutes another customer came up; Bill wandered off to the magazine rack, then returned.

We talked some more, he bought the book, and we became friends. Months later, Bill thought of me when he was called in on a job interview by the producers of a show we'll call *Ghostly Tales*. Because he knew me and my work, and wasn't interested in the job himself, he did say to them, before leaving, "You know, if you're doing shows in this supernatural arena, you really should talk to this friend of mine who's written a successful book about it."

That book had set the wheels in motion. One of the production execs, Carl, called my agent; my agent—flabbergasted, no doubt, that anyone wanted to meet me—called me, and the meeting was set.

See what I said about circuitous? But it worked. Never underestimate the power of these seemingly unrelated connections and friendships. My barber, I'm sure, would chalk it up to destiny.

■ ■ ■ Part VII

Making Hay

Catching a Break

■ ■ ■ My friend Bill had indeed cracked the door open, enough for me to get my foot in, but if I wanted to wedge the rest of my body in after it, I was going to have to do my homework.

In other words, I began the research process I've suggested *you* do. I taped the show, I studied the episode, I tried to get a copy of a sample script (but for one reason or another, didn't manage to do so in time for the meeting). Then I turned on my computer and opened what I call "My Brilliant Idea File."

If you don't have one of these, you should.

Into this file, I have always entered whatever good ideas cross my mind, regardless of whether or not I know what to do with them at the time. If I read an intriguing article in the paper, or see a story on the evening news, or come up with something in the course of a casual lunch conversation, I sit down at the keyboard and enter a few words, or paragraphs, about the idea, and maybe even a thought or two about where I could take it. Is it big enough to construct a novel around? Is it so topical that it would make a newspaper essay, and not much more? Does it lend itself to a short story, or to a movie script? If I don't know what to do with it, that doesn't matter. What does matter is that

I have some record of it that I can come back to later, at a time like this, when I need ideas fast.

A quick survey of the "Brilliant Idea" file revealed two possibilities. One was an idea about a sleep lab experiment gone awry, and another revolved around the Holy Grail. These were both ideas for which I had (one day) big plans—a movie script, a novel. But now, in extremis, with the meeting only forty-eight hours away, I immediately saw how they could be shaped and trimmed to fit the *Ghostly Tales* format.

I did just that, banging out a couple of pages on each one, just enough to introduce the main characters, the overall plot line, the resolution.

Then, as insurance, and because I can never leave well enough alone, I did a couple more stories, these tailored and built from the ground up expressly to suit what I perceived to be the *Ghostly Tales* story parameters.

My wife drew me my usual idiot's map to the meeting site ("turn left at the Foster Freeze, go six more blocks, enter the parking garage where the sign says, 'Parking Garage' . . .") and one hour earlier than a sane person would have bothered, I got in the car and left.

And here we learn that even the best preparation can leave you unprepared.

The guy I was meeting with, Carl, was a not untypical specimen of the young Hollywood exec—in crisp white shirt, dark tailored slacks, Italian loafers, and the ubiquitous phone headset, which allows a person to look you right in the eye while talking to someone else altogether. (I can't tell you the number of times I've started to reply, only to have the headset wearer raise a hand to hush me up so he can continue his meeting with the person he's really talking to. I'm just the schmuck who's sitting there.) If I could take all the headsets in Hollywood and twist them into one enormous coat hanger, I would.

It turned out the headset wasn't the biggest problem in this meeting. The problem was, I had come to the meeting, ably and well prepared to pitch . . . to the wrong show.

After I'd launched into my first idea, the one about the Holy Grail, Carl leaned back in his black leather chair and said, "I like it, but it's really more like *Dark World*, isn't it?"

"Dark World?" I thought. I didn't know what he was talking about. So of course I said, "I see exactly what you're saying. You're dead right." And moved on to my next idea, the one about the sleep lab.

When I was done pitching that one, which had been interrupted by two brief headset conversations (one involving hockey tickets, the other about a baby-sitter), Carl had the same reaction. "I don't know about this for *Ghostly Tales*—I don't think the idea is spooky enough, but it does sound like a *Dark World* kind of idea."

Dark World again? What was this guy going on about?

Well, I tried a third idea, got a similiar response (boy, did I apparently miss the *Ghostly Tales* boat) and I finally started to get the picture. The idea that there might be a *different* TV series under discussion here, one (for the purposes of this book) called *Dark World* came to me now like the beat of distant tom-toms— and only twenty or thirty minutes after anyone else sitting in my chair would have heard the sound.

Dark World. A new series. Why had no one told me?

As soon as Carl finished up with another headset conversation (the hockey tickets again), I cleared my throat and said, "So, this *Dark World* project . . . I think it sounds like a great idea."

"It is," Carl agreed.

"Ever since I heard about it, I've been dying to be involved."

"That's why we brought you in," Carl said. "Your book, *Fallen Angels*, is right on target."

"Oh, you have the book?"

He swiveled toward his desk, where I could now see the spine of the book behind a box of fat-free crackers. (Normally, I can smell one of my books at a hundred paces. My senses must have been altered by anxiety.)

"Of course, it's going to be very edgy," Carl explained.

"Absolutely."

"And very fresh," he added, "the characters, the setting, the stories."

"Is there anything else you can tell me about it?" I asked, and, instead of answering me directly, Carl punched a button on his phone console, spoke again into the air, and an assistant bustled in, carrying the materials he'd requested for me, which turned out to be a bible, a glossary, and some illustrations for the new series, *Dark World*—the series that I had been, however inadvertently, pitching to, but with some success.

On the way home, I had to wonder if perhaps I did my best work when I was completely clueless.

Opportunity in Chaos

■ ■ ■ It was one of those great opportunities that come to all of us once or twice in a lifetime, and on which we must immediately attempt to capitalize.

Here was a show—a new show, one without a full staff yet, without an established shape and tone, without a definite cast of characters, without even a standing set completed yet—and for once I had an inside line.

Remember what I said about pilots and new shows? And the opportunities for a writer to contribute his own ideas and, even more to the point, get a job on staff?

Well, here was my chance, but because I had never been on staff before, because I had never sold a one-hour series script, even now I was not seriously considered for a position on the writing staff.

Instead, I was able to wangle a job as technical consultant, at $750 per week. For that, I was expected to read over all the material other writers were submitting, the drafts of the two-hour pilot episode (which had been cobbled together by many hands), and pretty much be available to answer questions on black magic and the occult whenever they came up. Although it wasn't all that I might have hoped, it wasn't half bad.

Making Hay

For one thing, I didn't have to come in to the office; I could still sleep late, and all I really had to do was be around when someone called. More importantly, it was, however tangentially, a staff position. It put me on the inside of a show for the first time in my so-called career, it made me part of the team and privy to the development process of a TV series.

Better yet, my field of expertise, demonology and the occult, was a notoriously vague one. It's a field where, to be perfectly frank, there is seldom a right or definitive answer. I used to get urgent calls with questions like "Would a demon wear a hat to a party?"

I'd mull it over for a second, ask a follow-up like, "Well, are we talking about a party before or after Labor Day?" then offer up my considered judgment. "No, definitely not—demons wear hats only to winter affairs."

And that was that. Who could argue the point?

After a few weeks, though, as I read over the actual script pages that came my way, I did begin to feel a growing dissatisfaction with my limited role. The pages were not always good, and it wasn't just a question of getting the occult stuff right. That I could fix. The stories were sometimes unfocused, the characters unlikable, and the rules of the game unclear.

Even in a supernatural story—in fact, especially in a supernatural story—you must set up rules and then abide by them. In a universe in which anything can happen, where your creature can be killed and come back again over and over and over, with no rhyme or reason, the story quickly loses its dramatic impact. The audience soon learns that nothing matters, that no action has a definite consequence, and as a result they fast lose interest. It's why I've never been able to sit through those moronic *Friday the Thirteenth* or *Nightmare on Elm Street* movies, even though I have to admit millions of less persnickety people have. After Jason or Freddy has been seemingly dispatched for the umpteenth time, only to pop back up again like a jack-in-the-box, I have to say, who cares? This isn't scary, it's just repetitious.

And this show, unless they were careful, could run into those same problems. I would address some of these stickier questions as best I could, with carefully worded memos (which I was never sure got read), but by and large nobody wanted to hear anything from me except specific answers to the specific questions I'd been asked.

Until the right question happened to come along, and everything changed again.

I think of it as the "Stained Glass Window Incident," and it's the best example I can offer of doing your job, however limited it might be, so thoroughly that you get noticed and unavoidably tapped for something better.

To give you a rough idea of the show *Dark World*, it's about a group of computer geeks who investigate supernatural and paranormal occurrences. The investigators all live together in a renovated old church with a stained glass window overlooking the main staircase.

It seems that the time had come to build the stained glass window, and the set designer had called down from Toronto (where the show was to be shot each week) to ask what exactly this stained glass window should look like. What was it supposed to depict? A scene from the Bible? A medieval landscape? Was there one panel? two? three? Should there be a motto of some sort, maybe in Latin, set into the colored glass?

As technical consultant (a title that always made me think I should be giving advice on lens filters and camera setups, not Latin inscriptions and magic spells), it was my job to provide some guidance here. What I did, in TV terms, was so remarkable, so unheard-of, so revolutionary in concept and execution, that it changed my life and career virtually overnight.

I did research.

I didn't just make something up, I didn't call a friend, I didn't even go to the Internet with a general appeal. I opened . . . a book. A volume of the eleventh edition of the Encyclopedia Britannica, to be precise, which contained a lengthy and authoritative entry on the history of stained glass.

Based on that entry, I was able to submit a three- or four-page memo describing how the stained glass window, given its supposed age and provenance, should be designed (as a triptych), what it might depict (the story of Simon Magus), along with a few inscriptions, in Latin, which I borrowed from my scholarly sister-in-law and which might serve as mottoes for the group of investigators.

I faxed the pages into the Los Angeles office, wandered off for some lunch and a movie, and returned late that afternoon just in time to pick up my ringing phone. The connection wasn't great, I could tell it was a car phone, but I could hear well enough to know it was Brian, the main producer of the show.

My first reaction was, I'm being fired. Pessimism is as hard-wired into me as the urge to drink when I'm thirsty. But then, over the crackling static and the line that frequently went dead, only to recover a split second later, I could discern the foreign, but very welcome, sound of praise. Brian was telling me he liked—no, he loved!—the stained glass memo.

"I don't know much about you," he went on, as I imagined him piloting his sports car along the Pacific Coast Highway, "but Carl's told me you're the expert on this stuff, and those pages were fantastic."

I mumbled something suitably self-deprecating.

"But listen," he went on, "I want you to know, that anything you want to do on the show, I want you to do. Whatever you want to write, write. If you want to do scripts, do them."

I didn't know what to say.

"Talk to Carl about it," he said, the line breaking up worse than ever. "I think you can be a really important part of the show."

A car horn blared, there was a buzzing on the line, and I could faintly make out another "talk to Carl" and a "good-bye" before the phone went dead.

For a few seconds, I just sat there, staring out the window at the spire of the church across the street. No, I didn't have an epiphany, but I did finally have an eruption of joy. I went flying out of my little office and into the living room, where my wife was lying on the sofa, reading *Vogue*.

She knew something was up from the jig I was doing around the room.

"We win the lottery?" she asked.

And after a moment's thought, I said, "Yes! That's exactly right! We just won the lottery!"

Glory Days

This was the beginning of what I think of as my honeymoon at *Dark World*, the period of several months during which I was treated with kindness and respect, the era when I could do no wrong, when my voice was firm and bold, my opinions heeded, my head held high.

It's probably just as well that I didn't know what was to come, that I was to go in the space of a couple of TV seasons from golden boy to village idiot.

For now, I was enjoying myself. I went in to confer with Carl, who offered me one of his latest fat-free snacks (this from a guy who had less body fat on his entire person than I was carrying in my big toe) and we discussed that Holy Grail idea I'd had.

We altered and shaped it so that the story lent itself better to the present cast of characters in the show, and we built in a backstory about a doomed romance that pitted our villain against one of our stars. This was perhaps the first time (of countless to come) I was drilled on the importance of making the stories personal. It wasn't enough that they be imaginative or intellectually challenging—the stories had to be *about* the regulars in the show.

Anyway, I got my marching orders, went home, and cranked away, as hard and as fast as I could, on the script.

When I got it back, and had stopped reeling from the volume of notes splashed all over the pages, I did the second draft.

And that was that, or so I thought.

A week or two later, I got a call to come into the office for a meeting with Brian.

"Anything in particular on the agenda?" I asked the assistant on the phone.

"Not that I know of. It's just a general meeting."

But when I got there, it wasn't exactly what I'd call general. Carl wasn't there, nor were any of the writers who'd been working on the show. In fact, no one was there but me . . . and three of the partners in the company.

It was held in Brian's office, a nice place but not overly grand, with lots of glass, and posters from their successful movies on the walls. I sat down in an armchair and did a quick mental assessment of the situation.

I was either there for a ritual beheading, at which all the partners wanted to be present, or this was some kind of a job interview for something better than a position as technical consultant. My antennae went up.

First, I heard some nice things about my Holy Grail script, then we moved on to more general topics. As we talked, I got my first real idea of how this company was run, and by whom.

There were three principal partners and together they made a formidable team. Brian was the point man, an aggressive, voluble salesman, who always seemed to be in motion, making a deal, fielding a call, resolving some urgent problem.

Drew was a writer/director with long, light brown hair, big thoughtful eyes, and the most artistic demeanor of the three. With Drew, you had the impression he'd much rather be discussing film theory or mythic archetypes than production budgets or Hollywood politics.

Roxanne was the third, and to me the most mysterious partner. I never heard her utter more than three words in a row in my presence. Slender and intense, she sat quietly, keeping her own counsel, though I could tell the other two partners paid great attention to whatever small signals she gave off.

The signals, apparently, were auspicious. Brian led me through some broad questions about what I thought the show, still in its formative stages, should focus on, what kind of stories it should tell, what liberties (because at its inception it was on a premium cable channel) I thought it should take. I was winging it, make no mistake, but because I had nothing much to lose (even without this TV gig, I could pull in $750 a week) I was answering honestly, and energetically. The energy, I'll admit, came from a genuine excitement about the show. I'm a big fan of the supernatural, as four of my previous books attest, and with this show I felt that such stories, drawing on the rich lore of the occult, could finally make it onto the air. There wasn't any other show quite like it, nor had there been, and I thought *Dark World* could really make its mark.

My enthusiasm, I guess, made its own impression, and at a certain point I caught the three partners exchanging a glance. *I've passed muster*, I thought, though for what exactly I didn't know.

I found out when Drew and Roxanne excused themselves, shaking my hand on their way out and smiling. That left me with Brian, who suddenly asked me what I was doing, professionally.

"Well, when I'm not consulting for this show . . ."

"I know all about that," he said, hurrying me along. "But what do you do for a living? Do you write for other places? What do you *do*?"

After a lightning-quick internal deliberation (*should I make something up, and if so, what?*) I realized that I could not decide on the right kind of fabrication fast enough. So I opted, however reluctantly, for the truth. "I write for several magazines and a couple of newspapers. Book reviews. Profiles. Essays."

Brian waited, as if there had to be more to my life than that. It didn't sound like very much to me, either.

Then, I suddenly remembered that I was working on a new book. I blurted out that I was writing something called *Raising Hell*.

"What's that? A novel?"

"It's a nonfiction book."

"What about?"

"Well, it's subtitled 'A Concise History of the Black Arts—and Those Who Dared to Practice Them.' "

And that's what clinched it.

"I need to know," Brian said, "if you'll come on staff, full-time." He was eager and aggressive, but at the same time there was something touchingly uncertain in his expression, the look a teenage boy might have when he'd just gone out on a limb and asked a girl for a date.

I was nonplussed. This wasn't just sitting at home as a technical consultant, answering a phone or a fax now and then. This sounded like real employment, at an office, with secretaries, meetings, and, worst of all, responsibilities. I had spent my whole adult life fleeing from a genuine career, and now I was having one thrown right at me, and I didn't know how to duck. Even if I *had* known how, I didn't want to hurt Brian's feelings. He was saying he needed me, he wanted me, the *show* needed me. . . . Who was I to say no?

M‌y first call, when I left the office, was to my agent. I had to stop at a 7-Eleven and use the pay phone because, yes, I am the last person in L.A. not to have a car phone, but all I got was his voice-mail.

"I've been offered a staff job—a real job, everyday!—on *Dark World*," I burbled into the machine. "You'll be hearing from Brian later today. What do I do?"

Then, still in a panic, I decided to drive straight to my friend Bill's apartment, the guy who'd gotten me into this whole mess by recommending me in the first place. If he didn't know what to do next, who would?

All the way there, I was turning it over in my head. A job. Full-time. I'd have to set an alarm, maybe two, in the morning. I'd have to buy my own car. (At that moment, I was driving my wife's.) No one in my family had ever held a decent job—we were all slackers, artistes, idlers. What would they say? What would they think of me?

What would I think of myself?

No longer would I be the lone eagle, flying high, the brave little sailboat tacking to its own wind, the solitary author in a ratty cardigan, holed up in his attic study with a half-empty bottle of bourbon.

After I nearly ran over a pedestrian in a crosswalk, I got a grip.

Bill, thank God, was home, and as was our custom, we repaired to the friendly and familiar confines of Polly's Pie Shop on the corner. There, I spilled out my alarming tale.

Bill listened, nodded, then talked me down, the way a cop might ease out onto the ledge to reason with a jumper. Not all staff jobs, he explained, called for nine-to-five hours—or any hours at all, for that matter. "I was on a show once," he said, "where I came in about three hours a week. The rest of the time, I still worked from home."

This was what I needed to hear.

"Maybe you'll get an office with a sofa in it," he continued. "I did. You can take a nap whenever you want to."

More good news.

"And it's a TV show—it's only for, say, thirteen weeks, or however long the show actually manages to run. Most shows die a quick death."

Be still my heart.

Then he laid down the fearful dictum.

"But either way, you've got no choice—you have to take the job."

"I do?"

"Yes. These jobs are very hard to get. When you're offered one, you have to take it."

My spirits plummeted.

"And you'll make a lot of money."

Now I was really terrified.

My agent, when I spoke to him later, confirmed it. "They're offering you a job as a staff writer, at $2,500 a week."

That was definitely more than I was making as a freelance writer. More money, in fact, than I had ever made on a regular basis in my whole life. Suddenly, before I'd even taken the deal, much less a cent of their money, I was worried about the rise in my tax bracket. (It's a family trait—no matter how good the news, there's always a way to find something bad in it.)

"But what about if I just continued writing scripts for them, like the one I just did, while staying on as a technical consultant?"

The scripts paid so well (on that show, we were getting roughly twenty-five thousand dollars for each one) that I was very reluctant to give that up.

"What do you think you'll be doing on staff?" the agent asked, baffled at my reaction. "You'll be answering the same questions about the supernatural stuff that you've always been answering, and you'll be writing scripts for the show—more scripts than you'd ever be able to get as a freelancer or a consultant."

That's when the lightbulb started to glow. "But if I'm on staff, won't writing the scripts just be considered part of my job?"

"Yes, it will be," the agent patiently explained. "But you will still be paid for each script you write, while you're drawing your weekly salary."

And now the lightbulb was burning bright. "I will?"

"Yes. That's how it works in TV."

To this day, it strikes me as odd, but wonderful, that TV pays you a handsome salary every week, and then tops it off by paying you extra for what, in my mind, is what you're there to do in the first place—write scripts for the show. But that's how it works. (When I was briefly on staff as an editor at a couple of magazines, I was not only editing but writing material for the magazines, and, believe me, if I had asked for extra money for my essays and articles, I'd have been put on medical leave for a chemical imbalance.)

TV is its own world.

"They want you to start right away," the agent said. "What do you want me to tell them?" I could tell from his voice that he could hardly believe he even had to ask that last question.

I swallowed hard, and said, "Tell them . . . yes . . . I guess."

That's the kind of conviction I'm famous for.

■ ■ ■ **Part VIII**

Staff Life

An Office of One's Own

■ ■ ■ Just in case you were unaware of the interchange-ability, the mutability, the insignificance of TV writers as a whole, let me say that when I showed up for work, and I was shown to my new office—a spare little room with a view of an enclosed concrete courtyard—the signs of the last tenant were apparent everywhere.

On the desk, there was a legal pad with a half-finished sentence on it. The pen was lying beside it. The chair, I swear, was still warm. That guy I passed in the hallway on the way in, the one who shouted "Down?" at the people in the elevator—was he, I wondered, the writer who had just been canned to make way for me? Was this his office I had just usurped?

Against the wall there were a dozen boxes with different initials scrawled in red Magic Marker on the side of each one. These initials, I would come to know, belonged to other writers, who had worked on this and other shows even earlier, and whose few personal effects had been bundled into these boxes on their own sudden departures. To me, it felt like I was a prisoner of the Bastille, finding messages from previous prisoners in my cell, who had long since been led to the guillotine.

Outside my office door was a galley kitchen area, stocked with sugary treats and soda pop, anything that might give a flagging writer that extra burst of unhealthy energy. (These kitchens are a common feature at TV shows.) I was already calculating how I could smuggle out some of the treats each night—should I go with the Coke, or the microwave popcorn packets?—when the casting director, who worked in the same large suite of offices, said hello and introduced herself.

When I said I was a new writer on the show and started to introduce myself, she held up a hand and said, "Don't bother with the last name—you writers aren't around long enough to make it worth memorizing last names. Nice to know you."

As she walked away, I thought, *Maybe I should take the Coke* and *the popcorn packets. Who knows how many opportunities I'll have?*

M y first day on staff I showed up at eight twenty-five A.M. I'd been so nervous about oversleeping, or leaving too little time to get through the morning traffic, that I was awake at six, before my alarms had even had a chance to go off, and behind the wheel of the car forty minutes earlier than I'd planned.

One advantage? The underground garage was blissfully un-occupied. As I would only learn later, the office complex where the company was located had been carefully planned and built with too few parking places. Unless you were a big enough cheese to have your own assigned space (a loftiness I never achieved) you could either valet your car or cruise up and down the aisles for half an hour, looking for that rare open spot. Walking back to your car it was not uncommon to find yourself trailed by some other poor soul, willing to follow you in his own car down three levels, and halfway across the garage, in the hope of snagging your space.

Aboveground the place looked less like a TV and movie lot than an anonymous, well-groomed office park in White Plains. The place had no Hollywood glamour whatsoever. True, there were tennis courts, an outdoor fountain, some rolling green lawns, but going there I always felt like one of the Eloi in *The Time Machine*, wandering stupidly around in the sunshine until the Morlocks got around to blaring the horn for me to come inside and be turned into mulch.

If only I'd known it was a premonition.

That first day was the only time I showed up quite so early. As it turned out, the assistant, whose job it was to unlock the main doors to the office, hadn't even arrived yet.

The second day, I came in at nine sharp.

The third day, nine-thirty.

The fourth day, I sauntered in around ten. And guess what? The world didn't stop. No one noticed, no one cared.

I started to think, *This TV gig might work out after all.*

Because writers are deemed to be creative, and as a result not entirely grown-up, we are allowed some slack when it comes to things like office hours, work attire, even personal hygiene. (One writer used to make a practice of kicking off his moccasins as soon as we convened, and for the rest of us it became quite an elaborate dance to snare the chair farthest from wherever he'd plunked down.)

It's not that TV writers don't work, they do—it's just that their hours are fairly malleable. As long as the scripts get done on time, the notes attended to, the changes made, no one really cares if you did the work between nine and five, or midnight and dawn (my own most productive hours). What's important is that you take care of the work you've been assigned, whether it takes you one hour or ten . . . and that you give the impression you've been giving it your all.

To that end, I quickly learned certain office skills every TV staffer should know, most of them designed to make even the laziest sod look like an eager beaver.

For one thing, forget the energy shortage and all that—leave your office lights on all the time. The only reason to turn them off is if you have to take a nap and you can't find your sleep mask.

For another, leave your computer and monitor on, too. A screen-saver is fine, but for extra points, just leave a script up there, with the cursor still flashing in the middle of a line of dialogue.

If you've got a blackboard or greaseboard on your wall

(chances are, you will) periodically scribble all kinds of stuff on it, the more cryptic the better, along with stern admonitions to yourself such as "FIX THIS!" or "RAISE STAKES!" or "ACT BREAK???" Make it look like you are your own worst taskmaster.

Always leave your chair turned slightly away from your desk, so that if anyone, such as the show-runner, looks in, it appears that you've vacated your seat in a hurry, probably just to run to the kitchen to grab a cup of coffee.

You might even leave a jacket or sweater draped loosely across the back of the chair. This outer garment ploy is a good way of implying, whatever the hour, that you're still at the office. (Do change the garment occasionally.) On one especially lucky day, when I'd just dropped by to drop off a disk—at seven P.M.— and I'd gone into my private office to call my mother, I heard Carl, the executive producer, coming down the hall. I hung up instantly—everyone in my family understood not to take offense when I did that—and stared at my computer monitor, looking perturbed, as if by an irreconcilable plot problem.

"Still here?" Carl said, popping his head in the door.

I took a second to respond, as if so deeply immersed in my work I hadn't heard him. "Oh, right. Hi, Carl," I said, absently. "What time is it?"

"After seven."

"Really? Huh."

I let my eyes flit back to the screen, as if I couldn't quite bear to separate myself from it.

"Don't let me disturb you," Carl said softly as he withdrew.

"Yeah, thanks," I mumbled. "Sure."

I listened for the sound of his departing footfall, and when I was sure he was gone I hit the automatic redial. My mother picked up where she'd left off without so much as missing a beat.

Playing Well with Others

◼◼◼ While you can fudge your own hours to some extent, attendance at staff meetings is mandatory. Depending on the show, these meetings can be anything from a benign convocation of great minds to a terrifying ordeal by fire. I've had maybe *two* such convocations and *innumerable* ordeals, but I've never worked on a show where the meetings weren't held.

Being on staff at a TV show is a little like being part of a fighter squadron. Remember in those old movies, where the pilots would sit around while the wing commander with a pointer mapped out their next mission for them? You're one of the flyers, and you have about as much choice in terms of what you're going to do next as they did.

For many writers, what appeals to us about writing in the first place is the solitary, creative nature of it. We like sitting down and making something out of nothing, something that bears entirely our own imprint. But in TV, that's just not how it works. It's a collaborative medium. You're just one plane in the squadron, and nowhere is that brought home to you more than in the staff meetings.

At one show, though I was not technically part of the staff, I was invited to attend some of the story meetings, and I witnessed a very warm and collegial spirit. The show was run by a courtly, Southern gentleman, and he kept the room in a good and amiable frame of mind. Unfortunately, he also kept the staff there for hours, while he droned on with detailed accounts of his own personal life, his marriages, and assorted career travails. The staff took it well—what else could they do?—but I couldn't help but notice how many hours of their week were taken up in these endless meetings while the show struggled, mightily, to stay on schedule. When it fell behind, the show-runner grew morose and frustrated, and blamed it on the faulty work ethic of his staff. *They weren't fast enough, they didn't come up with enough story ideas, they wrote so ham-handedly that he had no choice but to redo each script himself.* . . . The staff eventually felt the weight of his disapproval and returned it, if not openly, in kind.

At *Dark World*, these staff meetings, held roughly once a week, were a cross between a pop quiz and a bonding exercise.

I showed up early for the first few I attended, got a good seat at the oblong black table, and had a legal pad in front of me with several episode ideas already sketched out. Usually presided over by Brian, the meetings were designed, at least in part it seemed, to get us all working together, on the same track, toward a common goal, one for all and all of that.

Brian would often lead off with a detailed critique of whatever episode was in the docket at that moment—the one that was next up on the schedule, or in the deepest trouble, as far as he was concerned. There was always that fearful moment when he would announce the title of a script, and if it was yours, you suddenly gripped the arms of your chair and braced yourself for the onslaught.

Not that it always came. If after the announcement, Brian made some favorable, or even innocuous, comment, the rest of the staff fell instantly in line, nodding their approval, mumbling laudatory comments, smiling at you. Brian was the Sun King and we were all his courtiers, doing nothing to incur his wrath, everything to curry favor. Never forget—TV is an enterprise that brings new meaning to the word *sycophancy*.

However, if Brian happened instead to voice some displeasure, if the copy of the script in front of him bore a blizzard of notes scrawled and scratched on the pages, the whole room could instantly turn against you, the wretched perpetrator of this affront. Suddenly this script, which up until a moment ago might have been liked quite well, was a dreadful mess, a rank and putrid affair that cast its distorted shadow over everyone else's work. If the room had had stones in it, they'd have undoubtedly been thrown.

More times than I care to admit, the stones would have been thrown at me. I made several beginner's mistakes, and if I can save you from making the same ones, my suffering will not have been in vain.

For one thing, it wasn't such a good idea to have all those episode ideas sketched out. What I thought made me look like a hardworking and valuable member of the team instead made me look, at least to the three or four other writers in the room, like a weasel trying to grab too many episodes, and too much money, for myself. My friend Bill (who, yes, had followed me onto the staff of the show) used to caution me to cool it.

There was also the unfortunate fact that Brian had, quite unintentionally, anointed me the fair-haired boy. For a short time, I think there was a perception among some of the other writers that I could do no wrong. Brian liked my ideas, he had brought me on staff without the experience and past credits that the others could display, and several times he asked me for my opinion of other, more senior, staffers' work. I was flattered that he asked, and I always tried to give him my honest and considered opinion.

It's a fine line you have to walk in TV, being proud of and defending your work, and at the same time being open to the criticism and comments of your fellow staff members. I'll admit to being a bit sensitive. I really do put my best effort into my work, and by the time I submit it to public perusal a good part of my ego is attached. It's not easy seeing it taken apart before your very eyes.

At many shows, there's a lot of unnecessary brutality at staff meetings, which I can put down to two things: For one, there is often a general atmosphere of rivalry and insecurity among the staff members. Many writers have already been through the mill, and they are not anxious to go through it again.

Secondly, many writers that I have met at various shows are not, I'm sorry to say, exactly top-drawer. Strangely, the higher you go up the pyramid, the more untalented they often become. One I met on a family drama must have once seen that famous photo of Hemingway writing on a sort of lectern while standing up, because he always made a point of leaving his office door open, so we could see him standing, in attack mode, while he wrote his scripts on a lectern. Other than that, there was no mistaking him for Hemingway.

Another, a sitcom writer yet, always went out of his way to tell people he was "an angry man," which I think he equated somehow with creativity; the anger, we were to assume, was the fire of his artistry, burning so hot it was beyond his control. For me at least, it was difficult to see what he was so angry about. He'd grown up in a nice Eastern suburb, gone to the finest schools, lived in a Malibu beach house. I can only surmise that he felt ill-used, his great gifts largely overlooked by the entertainment industry as a whole. I think he felt himself to be better than the shows that he was relegated to working on; from my perspective, however, he was functioning *way beyond* the scope of his talents. He should have been patting himself on the back; never had one man gone so far on so little.

Another guy, who'd held lofty positions at one dreary show after another, used to go out of his way to appear terrifically solicitous whenever we crossed paths. He liked to pull me aside and share nuggets of his hard-won craft. "After you've made your first pass at a scene," he once counseled, "throw it out. That's just your first instinct, and it's the easiest. Then go at it again, and throw that out, too. Dig deeper. Do it a third time, because only then are you really breaking new ground."

In retrospect, I think he was just trying to slow me up by having me write everything three times. That, or he was actually sharing with me the method he himself employed to arrive at the singularly unlikely plot lines and dialogue he had unfailingly produced over the course of his long career.

Finally, if you are laboring under the impression that staff meetings are places of intellectual give-and-take, where it is possible to debate what is right for the show, what works, what doesn't, in the spirit of civil discourse and even camaraderie, well, let's just say it *can* happen. Some shows do work that way. But at many others, I'm afraid, the law of the jungle prevails. During one barrage that was brought against me for writing a script that "lacked emotions for the actors to play," I made the fatal error of saying that I thought intellectual content—constructing a story around an intriguing and original concept—was also important.

You'd have thought I'd saluted the Antichrist.

By the time the senior writers on that staff were done with me, I was flat as a pancake, and I never uttered the words "intellectual content" in any meeting, on any show, ever again.

We Meet Again

■ ■ ■ Despite all the politicking and toadying that goes on at staff meetings, certain things do ultimately get addressed.

Staff meetings are *designed* to bring everyone in the show—or at least everyone in the room—up to speed, to make sure that they are all on the same page, as it were. At any given time, one script is being shot, one is being prepped (that is, the casting is being done, the locations found, the props built), and a couple of others are on deck.

Sometimes one script has to be moved back in the schedule, and another one quickly found to replace it. There are a host of different reasons that this can happen: The first script might simply need more work (not an uncommon problem) or it could be that the show-runner is looking for a certain actor, or director, who isn't available until a later date. Sometimes there are problems with location availability. On one episode I wrote, the shooting schedule had to be put back because we were planning to use a particular house and garden that another TV show wasn't yet done with.

Other times, regular cast members themselves have a conflict—a personal crisis, another engagement they have to do—and as a result an episode in which they figure prominently has to be switched with one where they have little or no screen time.

That's why running a TV show is such a complicated process. It's like keeping a dozen different balls in the air, including scripts in various stages of completion that can be moved up in the rotation or moved back on a moment's notice.

Not to mention all the episodes already shot and in one stage or another of postproduction, where editing, looping, and scoring have to be done. Fortunately, as a writer, you'll have little or nothing to do with these details, but if you plan to move up the ranks and one day become an executive producer or show-runner yourself, you might as well know what's waiting in the wings. In all fairness, it's the seemingly endless run of problems that need to be attended to, from network notes to badly lighted footage, that account for much of the harried, blunt, even exasperated demeanor of many senior TV producers.

And somewhere in all this, these same producers must also deal with the most basic creative and story-telling problems, because if those aren't handled right, all the rest is beside the point.

Ideally, staff meetings are also brainstorming sessions, where, if things go well and everyone's feeling relaxed and friendly and unthreatened, a story is broken. No, not damaged beyond repair (though I've seen it happen), but broken in the sense of laid out, plot point for plot point, beat for beat, act break for act break. On a well-run show, the whole staff pitches in freely and helpfully to iron out the problems, find the right scenes, build in the escalating tension (or on a sitcom, spiral the hilarity), with the ultimate goal of getting the most out of this idea, and this episode, that's humanly possible.

Then, when that's been done, when the road map is as complete as the staff can make it, the writer whose idea it was, or whose assignment it has become, is sent off to do the grunt work, to fill in the blanks, bridge the gaps, write the witty or compelling dialogue. It's not an easy task, but given that much of the early assembly has been done en masse, it's also not as hard as it looks. If you follow the map or outline fairly carefully, you may not get to your destination in record time, or in perfect shape—this first draft could still be sloppy or lopsided, melodramatic or unfunny—but it won't be altogether wrong. It'll just be a matter of patching and punching up, trimming and elaborating, and again, in an ideal universe, your fellow staffers will be your best help.

At that perfect staff meeting, your comrades will lovingly, gently pinpoint the remaining problems in the script, discuss them, arrive at answers or resolutions. On a well-run show, the producers will keep the atmosphere kind and respectful, and even amusing; I've been at sessions where my own scripts were being minutely dissected, and I still left the room with a smile on my face and a spring in my step. I was actually anxious to get right on it. How come? Because I never felt personally demeaned or assaulted, because I really felt that everyone in the room was doing his best to make the script *better*. Under those circumstances, I can take any amount of criticism; any writer worth his salt can.

What does strike me as astounding is how often this *isn't* the case. It's almost as if TV writers have no memory; they forget that, even though *you're* the one in the cross hairs right now, *they* will be there two weeks later. So many times, I've witnessed unnecessary roughness among writers critiquing another's work, and I've never understood it. Even if I did, I wouldn't forgive it. In the course of their daily lives, writers encounter enough routine difficulties, ranging from eternal job insecurity to frequent creative blocks, and if we can't see our way clear to treating each other with courtesy and respect, I don't see how we can expect anyone else to.

O Canada!

■ ■ ■ One development that's making it easier all the time for writers to treat each other uncivilly is the fact that they don't even know each other. They can work on the same show and not even be *physically* in the room together. This separation isn't happening much with comedies, which are easy and cheap enough to shoot on a soundstage somewhere in Burbank, but it *is* the case with many dramas that the filming is done somewhere else (most notably Canada—though Australia, New Zealand, and Mexico are getting into the act, too.) The writers on one show can live and work in two quite separate camps.

As a result, and this for instance was the case with *Dark World*, you have some staff members sitting around a table in L.A., and some others gathered around a similar table up in Toronto, with both groups talking to each other over a voice-box placed in the center of each table. Do I really have to explain why this doesn't work very well? That when you can't actually see each other, you can't read body language or facial expression? That you constantly find people from both places trying to talk at the same time, creating a buzz of confusion on the line? That when you do wish to address someone, you have to announce who *you* are first, then specifically say who you're now responding to?

In a laudable attempt to solve the problem, the producers at *Dark World*, for example, instituted what they thought was a high-tech solution—they set up a video link, a postcard-sized section of a computer monitor, which allowed each group of writers to see the the others. This, it was theorized, would allow us all to establish visual contact and interact in a more friendly and natural manner.

That was the theory.

In fact, I think it only made things worse, because now the writers couldn't sit around comfortably, sharing a look, or a quiet joke, with their own comrades in whatever room they were in. Instead, to facilitate the video image, we all had to sit in a neat row of director's chairs and bar stools, in front of a stationary camera, calling to mind, inevitably, "see no evil, hear no evil, speak no evil." We felt as much like monkeys as we looked. From that day forward, we could never see our compatriots up in Canada as anything other than blurry little Claymation figures—just as, no doubt, they saw us. Even the audio suffered. All in all, it was dismally reminiscent of the moon landing—a noble endeavor plagued by fuzzy reception.

If anything, the video link just threw into greater relief the division between the two camps of the writing staff. The writers stationed up in Canada felt, and with considerable justification, that they were carrying the brunt of the work, that they were the ones on the line each day, cranking out the production rewrites, dealing with the cast and whatever problems they had, living out of a suitcase (even if the suitcase *was* deposited at a snazzy downtown hotel).

And those of us stationed down here—stateside, as it were—felt as if we were one large step removed from the actual production of the show, forced to sit idly by while our work was shipped off to Canada and shot by unseen hands. The bifurcation of the staff, while it might have been unavoidable given that the show was shot in Canada, to my mind created a regrettable rift among the writers.

Once, I even went so far as to mention this to a studio exec who happened to be seated next to me on the plane. We were flying from Toronto to L.A., first-class as I recall. We had just been staying in beautifully appointed rooms at an expensive hotel, shuttled back and forth to the set in limousines and vans, we had dined on expense accounts at wonderful restaurants. We weren't the only ones; several of us had made this trip north, and several more would make it every week like clockwork for the rest of the season. I asked the exec, after running through this costly litany, if it really made sense, in financial terms alone (putting aside the question of what was good for the show artistically), to split everything up this way just to shoot it in Canada.

"Everything you've just mentioned," he said, referring to the limos and airfares and hotel tabs, "all of that, and more, we save on just one union contract." Then he quickly buried himself again in his John Grisham novel. God, how network brass must hate the fact that they have to deal with these hopelessly naive—and nosy!—creative types.

Canada, it is true, offers all kinds of fiscal benefits: The unions charge less, the exchange rates are favorable, the government kicks in all kinds of tax breaks if you use Canadian actors, directors, grips, you name it. More and more American shows are heading north for just these reasons. But I still contend, a voice crying in the wilderness, that many of these shows pay a cost, difficult to assess in strictly monetary terms, for the move. These dramas are supposed to take place in America, but they lose that authentic American flavor, they don't look or feel quite right. Ever notice how many shows meant to take place in the United States somehow share that same dark green, gloomy, coniferous Canadian backdrop? Or how many supposedly *Chicago* cops shout, "Come out of the hoose!" Or how often a *New York* street scene looks suspiciously clean, sterile, and smaller-scale—almost, my lord, as if we were looking at Vancouver?

Not only that, when the writing and production staff is away from home, much less when it's divided into two groups and communicating over voice-boxes and video links, it loses that sense of cohesion that only proximity, not only to each other but to the cast and the crew, can give. I can't even tell you the number of times we writers in L.A. had to redo a *Dark World* scene because, not being around the standing sets all day, we had no idea that the window in the church headquarters didn't

183

look out onto the garden, or the staircase had no landing, or the front driveway, which was supposed to be long and tree-lined, was in fact about six feet wide and not much longer than an Oldsmobile. (In other words, it was okay to write that there was a mysterious hearse parked in the porte cochere, but the bit about it barreling up the shady driveway was out.) Every time we made a blunder like this, you could just about hear the snickers from the guys up north.

If we'd all been working more closely, most of this could have been avoided. And the staff meetings would, I am firmly convinced, have gone a lot better.

Mine is the minority view, and a powerless one, to boot. So, until further notice, make sure you have your passport and your hockey stick handy. You may be needing them.

The Beginning of Wisdom

■ ■ ■ There were many surprises waiting for me once I got on staff—a Toshiba laptop computer with a thousand functions and features I could never learn how to use, an assistant named Matt who would patiently attempt, over and over again, to show me how to use those functions and features, a bottomless supply of Carnation Instant Cocoa mix (to which I became wildly addicted).

But the biggest surprise of all, I believe, was what I was expected to do all day. Before I actually had a staff job, and an office to perform it in, I had the idea that TV writers spent their days writing script after script after script, that they were just script-writing machines whose chief (sole?) duty was to keep the teleplay pages coming, so that the actors could keep acting, the directors directing, the sponsors advertising. I think I pictured the writing staff sort of like grimy sailors, shoveling coal into the roaring engines of a mighty ship to provide the power needed to keep the thing moving relentlessly forward, no matter how rough the seas.

So you can imagine my shock when I learned that most TV writers contribute, in the course of a twenty-two–episode season, one or two, maybe three, scripts. My friend Shari was on a very popular sitcom last season and got her name on exactly one and a half scripts. (The half because she collaborated on the second episode.) And this wasn't because her talents were at all in question: In fact, she was rehired, and promoted, on the same show for this coming season.

My friend Katherine was on a one-hour drama all last year, and she wrote two episodes. (Perhaps it was in her spare time that she wrote the pilot script that has just been picked up for production by a major network. Kudos to Katherine.)

On that same show, another well-respected staff writer, who sat one office over from Katherine, also scored two episodes, and no more.

If ever I mentioned to any of them that, in my first season on *Dark World*, I had contributed four episodes (which I never felt was exactly overtaxing my faculties), they would look at me with a mixture of envy and wonder—not at the great talents that such a feat implied (they knew me too well for that), but at the fact that I'd managed somehow, despite all the politics and etiquette of TV staff writing, to score that many episodes.

How had I done it? It wasn't that hard, but, as I learned, it was a bit unusual. But then, so was that show.

For one thing, the producers of *Dark World* were also relatively new to TV-series production, so I think they weren't aware of, or wisely did not care about, just how most shows are run. They didn't worry about who wrote how many episodes. They just wanted the stories, and to them it didn't matter one jot where they came from. I think, amazingly enough, that they, too, were under the impression that that was why they'd hired the writing staff in the first place. It was only over time, as the show settled into some of the common TV routines, that the procedure started to resemble other TV shows' more closely. But to their credit, I think the producers' first instincts were good and right—hire a staff and let 'em loose.

So, if a TV staff writer does indeed contribute no more than two or three episodes to a full season, what does he do all day? Does writing those few scripts truly take up so many months?

To some extent, yes. And here's why.

When you're a freelancer, and you're writing just one episode for a show, it's true that you have to go through several steps (pitching, outlining, first and second drafts) but that's all you do. Once you've done your second draft, you're history.

When you're on staff, however, the process can go on forever. Somehow, the fact that you're in the office, that you're accessible, visible, on salary, means that you can be diddled with indefinitely. Just passing a producer in a hallway can yield an offhand suggestion—"Say," he might remark, "I was just thinking, what if instead of Milwaukee, your story took place in Norway?"—that can send you back to the drawing board for another week.

Also, although there might be some Writers Guild guidelines about all this, I've never known a staff writer, myself included, who's said no when he was asked to do another draft of his script. At some point, they're not even called drafts anymore, they're just colored pages, as in blue or yellow or green. In fact, there's usually so many different versions that you run out of primary colors, and the pages attached to the script become saffron, pink, salmon, or goldenrod.

Since no one can be expected to read through all of these different versions each time just to find the changes that have been made, a common practice is to asterisk your script. That is, every time you change even so much as a word in a line of the script, an asterisk—also called an "auto-revision" mark— pops up in the far right margin. (Don't worry—every script program has this auto-revision function and does it for you.) That way, if the producer wants to read through your latest draft and see if you've followed his instructions—"I never said Norway; I said *Gal*way!"—he can simply flip through the pages (fuschia, celadon, puce), look for the asterisks, and read over only those lines. It's also your way of proving that you have indeed paid attention to his orders.

In slimier hands, the revision process can be used, subtly, against you. On one show, I worked under a more senior writer who undertook to do the rewrites on a script of mine. By the time the script came back, nearly every line in the script was asterisked, giving our mutual bosses the impression that my draft had been so inept that the senior writer had had to rewrite every line. In some cases, the change was a comma, or a syllable, but in many more, there was no change whatsoever. Nothing. Except for the telltale asterisk. It wasn't the first time he'd pulled this stunt, either. On my scripts, and other writers', too.

I tried to make the point to the executive producers that this senior writer either (a) was asterisking everything just to give the idea that he was doing yeoman service, turning our dross into his gold, or (b) didn't know how to work the auto-revision mark function on his computer program. I offered to have my assistant—who'd taught me—teach him, too, but the producers just looked at me like I was crazy.

Well, the next script I turned in made my point. In one scene, a character recites the Pledge of Allegiance. When the same senior writer came to do the rewrite, I'll be darned if those very lines didn't come back with an asterisk on every one. I showed this to our superiors and said, "Unless he's also rewritten the Pledge of Allegiance, he's just trying to make it look like everything the rest of us turn in is such a mess that he has to sit down and rewrite every single line."

My reward for uncovering this subterfuge?

They looked at me like I was crazy.

Producers, network execs, they don't want to be drawn into the petty squabbles and disagreements among the members of the writing staff. When you, the writer, complain about something, it's as if the butler is asking the duke to settle a spat among the scullery maids. The higher-ups don't want to know what goes on belowstairs; they don't really care, just so long as the soup is hot and the beds get made.

And anyway, writers, as everyone knows, are a notoriously quarrelsome lot.

Earning Your Keep

■ ■ ■ There is only one task more onerous than doing endless rewrites of your own scripts, and that is doing endless rewrites of someone else's. Rewrites frequently comprise a very large part of a staff writer's day, and sometimes a good part of the night, too.

Aside from his or her own scripts, each staff writer winds up taking on several of the other scripts that have come in, some from outsiders, and some from fellow staffers whom the producers, in all their wisdom, have decided are burnt out on their own scripts. (The latter are the ones that really require a careful approach. When you're rewriting the script from the woman in the next office, you have to remember two things: One, she is your comrade in arms; and two, she may wind up doing the rewrite on *your* next script.)

The outside scripts, the ones that have been done by freelancers, are easier to deal with, if for no other reason than the freelancer is nowhere to be seen. He's long since taken the money and run. Whatever changes you make to the script, he'll never see them, until the episode airs, and then he'll just be so happy that the thing made it onto the air at all that he would never think to complain.

Sometimes the script you inherit is in good shape, well written, well thought out, and all you really have to do is tinker with it. That's a blessing. You thank your lucky stars when you get one of those.

Such scripts are, admittedly, rare. Most of the time freelance scripts have problems, and the most common problem of them all is in catching the tone of the show. The overall story has already been vetted, so there's seldom too much trouble with that. Instead, it's the small things—the jokes a character might, or might not, make; the way a scene ends, with a hug, rather than a bang; the interaction between the regular cast members— these are the things that a freelancer will have trouble getting right. It's not even his fault; he doesn't live with the show, day in and day out, the way you do, nor does he know all of its idiosyncracies (the fact that one actor hates big words, for instance, or that another is uncomfortable with physical comedy). Nor is he aware (how could he be?) of the direction in which the show is moving; every show has an arc, which extends over the entire season, and only the staffers know what that arc looks like.

That's why I get so irritated by producers, and for that matter many established TV writers, who love to rag on freelancers. Not long ago, I was at an industry function where a hotshot TV writer was amusing a small circle of friends by describing a Writers Guild meeting at which the issue of freelancers was being earnestly discussed. The question was, Why aren't more freelancers able to get work?

"And that's when I lost it," the hotshot said, with an equally big smile, "and I started pounding the table and shouting, 'Because freelancers suck! Freelancers *suck*!' "

Despite the fact that several of the people surrounding him were freelancers, he got an obliging laugh, but not from me.

Today's show-runner is tomorrow's freelancer. And a lot of the people riding high today would do well to remember that. In the writing business, we're all hired hands; we may land on a hit show and hang on to it for years, but one day it's going to end and we're going to find ourselves back on the street, looking for that next gig . . . as a freelancer once again.

• • •

While even the best freelance script will need some fine-tuning, there are some that do need a major overhaul. And for you, the staff writer, that represents perhaps the hardest part of your job. Not only will you have to push and pull this recalcitrant material into some semblance of shape, you'll also get no great fame or fortune for doing so. The original writer's name will stay on the script, and your contributions, no matter how great, will remain unsung.

On one show, I was given a first draft of a script that had been sitting in the producer's drawer. I never did find out why the writer hadn't done a second draft, or for that matter why the producer had let the thing languish for months, but for whatever reasons it had been revived now and it became my responsibility.

And it was indeed a mess. Maybe that's why it had been put aside, because no one wanted to think too hard about what needed to be done with it. At its core, there was a fairly decent idea—not a particularly original idea, but a viable one, nonetheless—and after reading through it, I had to figure out how to preserve that idea and throw out everything else around it, including the dialogue, the characters, and the resolution. Nothing else worked . . . but now, it had to be made to.

I went at the job in a big way, adding whole subplots, inventing new characters, writing all new dialogue; I can safely say that there wasn't a single line of the original script left by the time I was done. In the producer's view, it had turned out so well that he sent it to some name actors—one of whom, an Academy Award nominee, accepted the lead role.

Of course, that was one of the best-produced and -performed scripts I've ever written, and the one script that's ever been nominated for a prestigious prize. When I saw it listed among the nominees, with the original writer's name attached and, of course, no mention of mine, I have to admit I felt a pang, and a strong one at that. But that, I knew, was how the game was played. You labored in anonymity, for the greater good of the show.

Staff Life

In a weird way, it was something of a relief when the thing didn't win. On the one hand, sure, it would have been nice if it had taken the prize, as an acknowledgment of my craft and all of that. On the other hand, I think it would have killed me.

An Inside Job

■ ■ ■ All the freelance work in the world can't offer you the benefits that being on staff at a show for even one season can.

Getting on staff is like being ushered behind the curtain concealing the Wizard of Oz. From the outside, a TV show can appear baffling and incomprehensible. How does it get put together, produced, written, on the air? How do all the pieces fit together, who does what, when, where, for how long? Who are all those people on the credit roll, and what do they all do?

Once you've been on staff, once you've been behind the curtain, you understand just how the illusions are created, how the show moves forward, inch by painful inch, what the various tasks are and who's got the responsibility for doing them.

Working on staff takes a lot of the mystery out of TV, and that in turn gives you a sense of freedom. You learn what you, as the writer, have to worry about, and what you don't. You also learn what an immense support staff there is, from set designers to music directors, whose job it is to help flesh out and bring to life your story. In other words, you ain't all alone out there.

But it's the writers' room where you live. And depending on the show, that room, that world, can be anything from blissful to hellish. I've worked on shows where the writing staff was sneaky and competitive, and every day you just tried to keep your head down, get the work done, and make it back home unscathed. At one such show, I never felt quite safe until I'd gotten back into my car in the company garage, locked the doors, turned on a Bob Dylan tape, and peeled out toward Wilshire Boulevard. When I got home, my wife and I would go for a long walk around the neighborhood just so I could vent.

I've also worked on shows where the staff got along famously, where everyone, from the show-runner to the lowliest writer on the totem pole, treated each other with respect and genuine friendship, where it was possible, without fearing the consequences, to suggest any idea, no matter how outlandish, or to test your own limits, writing as boldly and imaginatively as you'd ever done. Working on shows like that, with people you like and trust, is the ultimate prize in this business, and when you get it, you learn to appreciate and savor it, because you know it's not always the case.

But I've never worked on any show where it wasn't possible to learn something more about the craft (even if it was only what *not* to do), or where I haven't met at least one person I liked and from whom I was able to get some further insight into the business. A lot of the time, these people haven't been on the writing staff at all; they're people working in other departments, doing other things altogether, whether it's making costumes, building props, or directing. When you're on staff at a show, you have the opportunity to meet and talk to all of these people.

It's not uncommon, in fact, to be invited onto the set when an episode you've written is being shot. It can be very exciting to see the sets that have been constructed, the wardrobe that's been chosen, the locations, and, most important of all, the actors and actresses who have been selected to embody your characters and speak your lines. For me, that's always been the most interesting part of it all—hearing how an actor interprets and delivers the lines I've written. Yes, I've heard my words get mangled a bit now and then, but more often than not I've been amazed at the nuances a good actor can find, and the conviction he or she can bring to the words. In a way, that's the trial by fire for your script—can the actors find in your words the character you intended, and bring that character to life on the screen?

If they can, that's fantastic. If they can't, it may be their fault, or it may be yours. You may have written the character less crisply than you thought. Although it's probably too late in the day to change anything on this particular script, you may be able to learn something from this misfire that keeps you on target in future.

The one thing you absolutely, positively, don't want to do, no matter how badly you think things are going, is approach an actor on the set, and give him instructions on how to read the line, alter his inflection, adjust his accent. If you do, the sane, reasonable actors will simply look you in the eye, nod, and pay no attention; the others might sock you. Actors and actresses, if you weren't already aware, are a tetchy lot and they don't take kindly to intervention.

If you really can't stand it, if you feel that you *must* correct some misinterpretation, or mispronunciation, then take the director aside, or the show-runner if he's around and it makes you more comfortable, and tell him your concern. Then leave it alone.

Not long ago, on a set where they were filming a show I'd written, a lead actor kept referring to one of the villains as a Russian "nationalist," instead of simply a Russian "national," as it was written. And, of course, there's a difference—one's a patriot, the other's just a citizen of Russia. I mentioned it to the show-runner, who mentioned it to the director, who mentioned it to the actor, who said, "Yeah, sure, no problem."

Then, he proceeded to say it his way—nationalist—in every subsequent take.

And no one, myself included, dared to bring it to his attention again.

Score one for the thespians.

On another show, I found that the lead actress, though beautiful, talented, and temperamental, also had a propensity for rendering the lines her own. In other words, she "interpreted" the dialogue, getting the gist of it across, but in her own words, and never exactly the same words in two consecutive takes. I could live with it most of the time. I sat in the shadows on my canvas stool, just trying to make sure she got the *sense* of each speech across each time, but there was one particular patch of dialogue where it was vitally important she end with two words, "the bridge." She was supposed to say something like, "We'll meet again, at the bridge." The bridge was the central metaphor of the story; it was even the title of the story, and it set up the next time, the *last* time, that the two main characters would meet—on the bridge.

I could not get her to say it. Every time she did the scene, she'd say something like, "I'll meet you there," or "I know where I will find you," or "We shall meet at our usual place." I don't know what it was about the words "the bridge" that she just couldn't bear to say, but the more the director, the executive producer, even I, tried to get her to say it, the more she resisted. She didn't even have a reason. She'd say she was going to do it, the cameras would roll, and we'd be right back where we started, with her saying something like, "I'll meet you there, above the river."

Finally, we took a huddle out of her earshot, and I said, "Here's what we do. We turn the lines around, so that it's the other actor who says they'll meet up at the bridge. She already knows how important it is, how that's the emotional thrust of the scene and the camera's going to hold on the face of the person who's just said it. Let's see what she does when she gets the rewrite."

I raced to my laptop, adjusted the scene so that the other character brought up the bridge (it wasn't as effective, but we were out of ideas), and then I handed them the new dialogue.

The director cleverly focused on the other actor like a laser beam, bringing home to him how *critical* these lines were, how pregnant with meaning, how expressively he should emote them.

As he did so, the actress stood there thunderstruck, her lips apart, the color draining from her face, the page of new dialogue crumpling in her fist.

"No, no, no, no, no," she finally blurted out. "The scene doesn't work this way at all."

She returned to her mark, tossed the new page off the set, and impatiently declared, "Let's go already. I don't know why this one little scene should be taking so long."

The director shot a glance at the other actor—*do it the old way*—then at me. He called for action, the camera rolled, and the actress did the scene letter perfect, ending with the line, "We'll meet again, at the bridge."

Score one for the writers.

Casting a Wide Net

■ ■ ■ Maybe it's because writers get kicked as often as they do, and seldom have anybody to kick back, that they like to make light of actors. Lord knows, it's easy to do.

On one show, we had a lead actress who actually took a tape measure to her trailer and then to the male lead's trailer, and threw a fit when she discovered that his was several inches longer than hers.

On that same show, another cast member actually objected to getting *so many* lines. (This is *not* the usual complaint from actors.) He hated having to memorize so many words, and wondered if we couldn't shave back his dialogue a bit. The other cast members were only too happy to pick up the slack.

One "famous" actress (though not nearly as famous as she thought) would only do one take, and refused to cooperate with any of the publicity stuff—interviews and photo ops—that the show desperately needed to boost its ratings. (Hey, she was only earning in the mid–six figures, for about eight weeks' work; why should she be expected to pitch in like that?)

Are actors and actresses the numskulls we like to make them out to be?

Sometimes.

Are they petty tyrants, spoiled rotten and full of themselves?
Sometimes.
Are they strutting egos, overpaid and undereducated?
Sometimes.
But for a writer, there is nothing so instructive, nothing so
well calculated to engender understanding, and even sympathy,
for the acting corps, as attending a casting session. I always recommend it highly to every writer I know. If you're invited to sit
in (and you aren't always), jump at the chance. If you're *not*
invited, but you think you might get a yes if you ask, then ask.
Trust me—it'll be interesting, it'll be informative, and it's guaranteed to leave you feeling, for one reason and one reason alone,
glad that you're a writer: You don't have to come in for cattle
calls.

On audition day, you'll find a bullpen, or waiting area, filled
with actors who look vaguely alike. Maybe they're all willowy,
blond women, up for the role of the young heiress, or distinguished, gray-haired men, up for the bank president. I remember
with special amusement the day I walked in on a whole room
packed with swarthy, middle-aged men, there to audition for the
mob hit man. These guys looked like they'd come straight from
Little Italy, but when I sat down nearby and listened in on their
conversation, what I heard was a heated debate about the Venice
Biennale, followed by perceptive critiques of a Tennessee Wil-
liams revival and the plans to rebuild the Globe theater.

Serves me right for judging the books by their covers.

What I learned to appreciate over time was the incredible
bravery and resilience that actors and actresses need, just to go
out each day and do what they do. Or, I should say, to get the
opportunity to do what they do. While a writer can hole up with
a legal pad and a pen, and write whatever, whenever, wherever
he wants, actors can't. They need lines, a stage, a camera, to
practice their art, and to get those things, they have to pass an
audition first.

Each show works with a casting director, whose job it is to
find the right people for all the various parts, big and small, that

199

come up in any given episode. When it comes time to cast a role, the casting director flips through her voluminous files of head shots and stacks of videotapes, and then calls in anywhere from two to two dozen actors or actresses who fit the general parameters of the character.

That, incidentally, is why, when you read (or write) a script, the characters are usually described in only the most minimal terms—tall, short, white, black, old, young. The first few times I read scripts, I just thought the writers were being lazy, but there's a reason for doing this, and the reason is, you want to be sure that a variety of actors could fill the role. When you're writing a description of a character, you want to mention only those features that are really essential, enough to give the reader an impression of who the person is, but not down to every last detail. If it matters that the seductive teacher is blond, then say she's a blond; if the point is only that she's attractive, then just say that.

Personally, I favor just the briefest of physical descriptions, accompanied perhaps by a phrase that tells us something about who the person is: "a guy who looks like he'd sooner starve— and he is starving—than ask for a handout." Whatever. Just something that gives us a quick take on his personality, not his height and weight. Actors and actresses can't do much about how tall they are, but the good ones will all know how to interpret a character who's lost everything but his pride. That's the kind of assignment they relish.

You'll also be amazed, when you see different actors auditioning for a role you've written, what a wide variety of types can fill the bill. In your mind's eye, you may have seen an oily little guy in the role, but then the next thing you know a big, heavy actor has blown you away with his reading. Look at *Death of a Salesman*, to cite just one of the most famous examples. Dustin Hoffman brought Willy Loman to life on Broadway as a small, agitated, overeager dreamer; a decade later, the burly, boisterous Brian Dennehy played the part to equal acclaim. They weren't playing a *physical* part, they were playing a person, someone whose life and hopes had dried up, a traveling salesman who never understood what had hit him.

On one show I'd written, we were auditioning an actor I'd seen in several comedies, but this time it was for the part of a petty thief. He came in, gave a great reading, and was already on his way out of the room when the show-runner had a thought and said, "You wouldn't want to read for the part of the criminal mastermind, would you?" The actor, though caught off-guard, of course agreed; he was given the appropriate pages to read over, and ten minutes later he came back into the room, and this time, instead of playing a low-life crook, he was now the crook's sleek and sophisticated, foreign-born boss. He was so persuasive that the hard decision had to be made: which role to cast him in. Since the thief was easier to cast, we decided to let that part go to someone else, and we kept the actor for the more demanding role of the mastermind.

Was he the type I'd had in mind when I wrote that character? Not one bit. I'd been picturing a lean, dissolute English aristocrat, and the man we'd just chosen was an olive-skinned, Latin man with a big, fleshy nose and wet brown eyes. Could he play clever, classy, and dangerously charming? To a T.

The dangers of writing stereotypes rather than characters was brought home to me, in a strange way, when we were casting for the part of an Egyptian professor, an expert on mummy preservation. The word went out from the casting director, and sure enough a dozen actors of Middle Eastern origin showed up, but it was only as the auditions continued that I started to grow uncomfortable, and it wasn't because of the chair I was sitting in.

The room was the usual setup. I sat on one side of a long table with the show-runner, the director, and a casting agent. Behind us, manned by one of the assistants, was a small camera on a tripod, which we used to record the auditions. (Sometimes you really don't know what you've got till you watch the videotaped performance later on.) On the other side of the table, a chair was placed in front of the camera.

Each actor came in, clutching his "sides" (the page or two of dialogue that each of them reads from for the audition), sat down, and before he did the read-through with the casting agent playing the other part, we did the obligatory minute or so of chitchat.

The first guy turned out to be a Stanford graduate, whose last acting job was as "a terrorist who hijacks a school bus."

The second guy had trained at Juilliard, and his last gig was playing "the terrorist who was sucked out the airplane door" on a recently released big-budget action-adventure.

The third played "a Muslim terrorist in a TV movie-of-the-week, who plants a bomb in the New York City subway."

You get the picture, and there were about six more of these guys to come, each one with the same story. All of them articulate, well-trained, rarin'-to-go actors, and every part they'd played—in some cases, the *only* parts they'd played—had been Arab terrorists. You can't imagine how grateful, and anxious, they were to play this part, a respectable Egyptian professor, the first part they'd been offered for months where they didn't have to hold a gun to someone's head, or shout, "Allah be praised!" I was pleased about that, and only sorry that out of the four actors who gave really great readings, only one could get the role.

It also made me aware—and I promise to get off of this soapbox as quickly as I've gotten on it—how easy it is to write the stereotypes, to cast people in limited roles, rather than *reaching* just a little, to imagine something different. It reminded me, when writing my own scripts or books, to think through what might seem to be my most unchallenged decisions, the ones that came too easily, and question if they were really right, or simply expedient. Yes, if I need an Arab terrorist for a story, I'll write one, but I'll think twice about why I made that call.

Finally, by attending casting sessions, I got the chance to see just one more piece of evidence to support the theory that, no matter what TV people say, no matter how loudly they protest, they're still in thrall to the feature world. All the money in the world, and all the viewers, will never quite ease this deep-seated inferiority complex that TV people have when it comes to the movies.

We were casting for the part of a brilliant, and of course beautiful, grad student at Harvard. Out of the ten women who auditioned, one was absolutely on the mark. She was not only pretty, she had a very incisive way of speaking and a very smart glint in her eye that really made her convincing as a scholar. I thought, and so did the others in the room, that she had clinched the part the minute her audition was done.

But the next actress ushered in by the casting director had been . . . *in a movie*! A box-office hit! True, she'd been onscreen about forty-five seconds, had delivered three lines, and had never been seen again, but she'd been in a *feature*. While her reading was okay, it was not nearly as good as the other actress's had been, nor did she look for one second like someone who could possibly have been buried in books much of her life. (Whipped cream, maybe.) I put in my two cents' worth arguing for the other actress, but we all know the kind of weight a writer throws around. The movie actress got the part, and that was that.

So I guess I was less than sympathetic when I started to get reports back from the set that their choice was behaving, to everyone's astonishment . . . like a movie actress! She wasn't satisfied with her hotel room, she never got to the set on time, she didn't get along with the other actors, and she wasn't really very convincing as a grad student at Harvard.

Well, duh.

Hard Lesson #1: Shut Up

■ ■ ■ Strangely enough, working on a TV staff taught me two diametrically opposed things.

The first of these things was: Just shut up and get on with it. That lesson was brought home to me by the Great Asterisk Fiasco mentioned earlier (why did I think the producers would care if one writer was trying to make the others look bad?) and a hundred other such skirmishes and defeats.

Almost no problem in TV is so great that it's worth tying yourself into knots over. You do what you can, and you move on. It's TV, okay? People are watching it while they heat their microwave dinners, floss their teeth, and cut coupons out of the paper.

Nor can you do much about the way the TV industry runs. Even if the scripting process seems to you, as it does to me, byzantine and redundant, there is nothing you can do to change it—until you get that big gig running the network.

If the established method is to write a zillion drafts, changing things backward and forward, forward and back, taking contradictory notes from a dozen different producers, losing the credit for things you've done right, unfairly taking the blame for things that have gone wrong, rewriting strong concepts until they're weak, sharp dialogue until it's dull, rounded characters until they're flattened by the weight of revision, then that's just the way it is, and the sooner you, and I, get with the program—literally and figuratively—the better off we'll be.

Depending on how you choose to look at it, the nadir, or the zenith, of my TV writing career came one day in an executive's office when he said, "Have I told you my new idea for your script?" and I, without missing a beat, earnestly replied, "No, but I like it a lot."

The words were out of my mouth before I'd even had time to consider them, or to see the bleak humor. Not surprisingly, the exec saw nothing funny in them either. Without missing a beat himself, he proceeded to tell me his new idea, which turned out, of course, to be some absolutely harebrained notion that had popped into his head while he was working out on the StairMaster that morning. To the best of my recollection, it had something to do with two of the series regulars discovering, quite by chance, that one of their ancestors had burned one of the other's at the stake—*accidentally*—years before. Wow, that's gotta leave some unresolved issues for the later generations to explore.

As I sat there, dutifully jotting down this brilliant aperçu, I recognized that I had just crossed the Rubicon. Although I had until then shaken my head, even sneered, at the craven behavior of so many of my fellow TV writers—those yes-men who rolled over at the first stupid suggestion from some network exec or show-runner, terrified of losing their cushy berth—at that moment, I knew those days were gone. I had just become one of them.

On the bright side, which I tried desperately to see on the way home that night, I told myself that I had managed, for the first time, to abandon all ego when it came to my work. I was now the team player that so many of the most successful TV writers appeared to be. They could turn on a dime, and keep right on going. If the producer didn't like the urban setting, they'd instantly make it rural. If he didn't like the dog, it became a cat. Night brightened into day, Minnesota became Miami, senior citizens turned into teenagers. (*Everyone* turned into teenagers.) The hallmark of a TV pro was his or her ability to take the hits, the crazy changes, the nonsensical notes, the scrambled directives, and simply sit down and do them, as well as they could possibly be done. There was actually something noble, something impressive, in that—or so I told myself now—something I didn't have to be ashamed of. TV writers are seldom in a position to stand up and fight for what they believe in, or for what they have written—it ain't their show—but when it comes to ingenuity, they are second to none.

Hard Lesson #2: Speak Up

■■■ Around the same time that I learned to shut up and do what I was asked, I also learned that second, and somewhat contradictory, lesson. (Haven't we been told, by no less than F. Scott Fitzgerald, that "the test of a first-rate intelligence is the ability to hold two opposed ideas in the mind at the same time, and still retain the ability to function"?) I learned that in TV you do have to speak up for yourself, stake your claim to what's due you, and defend your own interests, because there's no shortage of unscrupulous sorts who will try to take the credit for your good work, lay the blame on you for whatever goes bad, and when the opportunity presents itself divert the dough from your pocket to their own.

Does that sound harsh? Admittedly.

Is it true? Unfortunately.

In TV writing, a lot of money is at stake, and sometimes it's over things that you never even knew were valuable. But the pros know, and before you can say "Wait a second—that's mine," they can cut you out of your fair share.

Case in point: On one show I wrote for, the producers decided to do what's called a "clip show" for the final episode of the season. That's a fairly common practice, and all it means is that rather than trying to find the money to produce another complete original episode (budgets often run out before the season does), the producers have elected to concoct a fairly thin story line that will allow them to paste together a final episode largely by lifting bits and pieces from previous episodes and running them as flashbacks.

In this particular case, the two writer/producers in charge of the clip show put together an episode that was remarkable for two reasons: one was its sheer stupidity, excessive even by the standards of this admittedly dim-witted program, and the other was its audacity, judged even by the low ethical standards of TV. Almost the entire clip show was made up of fragments from the work of these two writers themselves, one of whom had only come onto the show in midseason and whose contribution to the show comprised in its entirety one dreadful episode. One of the other staff writers, who'd written several of the better episodes of the show, screamed bloody murder when he first caught a glimpse of this mess, and to placate him the two miscreants immediately slotted a few minutes of his clips into the show.

Unfortunately, to make room for them, they wound up taking out the few seconds of screen time my own work, and that of a few other writers, had barely managed to rack up. You could bet your bottom dollar that they wouldn't take out a millisecond of the clips drawn from their own episodes, and not just because they loved and believed in their own work.

What they really believed in was the money. According to a complex formula, which only the wizards at the Writers Guild can calculate, the script fee for a clip show is divided up among all the writers whose work is included, and it's based on how many minutes and seconds of screen time each writer's work represents. So, clearly, if ten minutes of clips in the show are drawn from your episodes, you're going to do a lot better than the guy with ten seconds.

In an ideal world, the writers in charge of shaping the clip show would look back over the season, pick out the best moments and scenes, and do their best to make sure that all the writers who had worked on the show were well and fairly represented. It would be the intelligent, the right, the honorable thing to do.

For those reasons alone, it doesn't stand a chance.

Then there's the "new character" gambit, also quite popular. Here's how that one works.

You write an episode of the show, in which a new character, never before seen on camera, makes his appearance. Let's say he's a bodyguard for the hero. Everybody from the producers to the show's at-home audience falls in love with this guy. The actor who plays him gets a contract to appear in the rest of the episodes for that season. And do you know what that means for you?

Character payments.

Every time that character appears in a later episode, whether it's this season, next season, ten seasons down the line, you get a small, but nonetheless pleasant, payment. Even if you weren't aware of this practice, trust me—the veterans on the show are; and they may well try to take it from you. Before I knew the score, I got zapped.

On one show, I wrote in the character of a housekeeper for the heroine. Someone to serve in that capacity was clearly needed in the show on an ongoing basis. I called her Sonja, and she was of Eastern European origins. Well, when the script came back from the rewrite factory, she was now Monica, from Western Europe. Damned if she hadn't just landed, like a refugee leaping from the dock at the last second, on the deck of the show-runner's script, which was just then going before the cameras.

In other words, *before* mine.

To no one's surprise, Monica, though she was as colorless and hackneyed as all the characters created by this writer, hung in there bravely for the rest of the season and, last I heard, she's still going strong. And the show-runner, have no doubt, is cashing his character payments regularly.

• • •

Staff Life

To make your voice heard in TV, you can't be overly modest, shy, or polite. If you feel like a scam is being run on you, chances are, it is, and unless you holler, that scam will succeed. Somebody else will be cashing your character payments, erasing your clips to make room for their own, or claiming episode slots that by rights should have been yours.

In the sitcom staff meetings, things can get pretty boisterous, with everyone wildly pitching ideas, jokes, gags, and bits and trying, more often than not, to top the one that just got a laugh. You get no points for courtesy on a sitcom staff.

On dramas, the room may be comparatively more sedate, but you've still got to get in there and mix it up a bit. You may get bruised, and even do some bruising yourself, but you've got to participate. Do you remember, for instance, those soccer games in junior high? It didn't take long for you, and everyone else on the team, to figure out which of your players always managed to stay just a few feet *away* from all the kicking and running, who gave the *appearance* of playing while actually staying clear of all those flying feet and jostling shoulders.

And that was not a player you picked again, the next time it came to choosing up sides.

Think of the staff meeting as a scrimmage. Get in there, and expect to come out dirty.

Taking Credit

For someone trained from birth to avoid confrontation, the prospect of a script arbitration—basically, an argument over who should receive credit for what—was about the last thing in the world I ever wanted to engage in. But that didn't keep it from happening.

Unfortunately, into every TV writer's life, at some point an arbitration will fall. And much as you might wish to avoid it, the only alternative is to roll over and play dead (which was my first inclination), but in the long run that reaction is an unwise one and unnecessary.

An arbitration may be a headache, but it's not a fatal disease. There are basically two ways it can get started.

Way number one: Let's say you've worked on a script in one capacity or another—maybe you created the story, but somebody else actually got to write the teleplay—and then you get the Notice of Tentative Writing Credits (the NTWC, as it is sometimes denoted) and all it says is "Written by the Other Person."

You have, as discussed earlier in this very book, a brief period of time, five or ten days, to lodge a complaint with the Writers Guild, saying in essence, "Hold on there—I may not be the one who wrote the actual teleplay, but I *am* the one who wrote the story and outline," thereby starting an arbitration proceeding.

Conversely, and this is way number two, you can be merrily going about your business, whistling a happy tune, when you get word that *someone else*—no doubt some undeserving, grasping soul—has laid claim to some portion of *your* story or script!

That's what happened to me.

I had written one freelance episode of a show, and it had gone so well that the producers called me in to do another. But for this one, they already had their own high-concept that they wanted to do; they shared their idea with me, along with the fact that another writer, Sally, had been working on it. They gave me the outline she'd written, an outline they had already, and summarily, rejected.

I could see why. It took the basic premise of their story and went way off in left field with it. I'm not knocking Sally for that outline; for all I know, she was just following, as best she could, the confusing instructions she'd received from the two produc-ers, and these two were more than capable—no, they were pos-itively unsurpassed—at issuing confused instructions.

So when I decided to embark on this same project, I wanted to be as clear as possible on where we were starting, and where we were going. My first call was to the producers. I began, in typical TV-writer mode, by complimenting them on the excel-lence of their conception, the deep insight and sensitivity it dis-played, the startling originality of the whole endeavor. (They'd seen an old movie on AMC and decided to rip it off.)

They disagreed with none of my praise. Then I told them, "If it's okay with you, I'd like to discard this previous outline altogether."

"We already have," they replied.

"Fine. Because what I want to do is go off in another direction entirely."

"Great. That's exactly what we want. That's why we called you."

"Okay," I went on, cautiously, "here's what I think we should do with this idea." I proceeded to sketch in the general arc of the story I was proposing and, to my relief, they immediately went for it.

Not that everything went smoothly from that point forward.

I wrote up my idea in a six-page, single-spaced outline, which came back with notes all over it and became a nine-page outline, which came back again and then became an eleven-page outline, and so on. Eventually we did arrive at the point where everyone was so heartily sick of outlines that I was allowed to go to script.

I wrote the script, turned it in, went through a couple of more drafts (one of which was, by guild standards, probably unrequired), and then retired from this particular fray. The script was handed over to the staff to put it into production.

I remained retired until I got word, out of the blue, that the credits notification had been challenged, and that Sally, the writer of that first outline, was now asking for shared story credit. Never having been in this situation before, I was puzzled as to what to do and, stupidly, I asked the producers.

Their reaction was interesting. As one of them put it, "Well, Sally is a very well known TV writer, you know. Lots of credits, on very high-profile shows."

Yeah, so? I didn't know how this was relevant.

"And we did ask her to work on that outline for us," he added.

"Was she paid for it?" I asked.

"Oh, yes. Of course."

Now my mind was at rest, at least on that score.

"Why don't you just share the credit and let it go?" the producer continued. "She's been a friend of ours for years."

"Yeah," said the other, "it's no big deal. Let it go."

And in the interest of being a team player, in proving my magnanimity, in showing everyone just what a sport I could be, I thought, *Okay, I'll just let it slide. Hey, it'll do me good in the long run, because now that these producers have seen what a class act I am, they'll reward me with more work in the future.*

And then I tried to go to sleep that night.

Why, I found myself wondering around three A.M., *was I giving away something I didn't feel this other person was entitled to receive? Why was I allowing someone I had never met, who'd already been paid for her own work, to share the money that would be due for mine?* (At this point, I didn't even know exactly what Sally's share of the fees would be, but I knew it would be something.) *Why was I going to share the credit for a story I had come up with—using my own, and only my own, overtaxed faculties—with somebody else who'd essentially been handed the same assignment and bungled it?*

And why (now that I was dwelling on it over a bowl of cold cereal at three-thirty A.M.) *did this Sally person—who already had a ton of credits, and money—think she could just stroll in and lay claim to some of my work? For her, one more story credit was neither here nor there. For me, it was a big deal.*

The next day, I timidly brought up the subject with one of the producers, who looked baffled that this problem—this *trifle*— was coming up again. "Sally's my friend, okay?" he said. "We plan to work with her again."

"Yes, I see that, I understand, but as we all agreed at the outset, I wasn't going to use anything from the outline she'd done."

"You're still pretty new to this business, so let me give you a piece of advice. You don't want to go around alienating people like Sally. She knows everybody. Let her have the story credit."

End of discussion . . . but not the end of my ruminations. There was just something about that suggestion of his, not to alienate someone who'd already made her bones in the business, that stuck in my craw. Right along with the notion that, because Sally and the producers were friends, I should be the one to roll over. If everyone was so friendly, and everyone was already so accomplished and successful, then why did they all feel the right thing to do was to poach on my own hard-won episode?

I called my agent for advice, told him the whole story, and asked him for his take on the consequences—pro and con—of challenging Sally's demand. What would I risk, I wanted to know, by asking for an arbitration—the producer's good will? Future asignments? An invitation to Sally's next barbecue? What would I win if I *prevailed* in an arbitration?

And, because agents are nothing if not vague, he proceeded to outline in muddy and uncertain terms what he believed the fallout either way would be. There would be advantages, a bit more money for me; and disadvantages, the headache, the ill will. The bottom line, as he was wont to put it, was that I should probably not bother with the arbitration.

"Really?" I asked. "You think I should just let it go?"

"I would. I mean, I'm friends with your producers—our agency represents them—and this is really no big deal. Let them have it their way."

Friends again. It began to seem like everyone in this town was friends with each other, and until I too had attained that lofty status, I should just be nice and give away the farm.

But when I thought about that, I realized that I already *had* friends—a lot of them, and good ones at that. I also realized that these people, these *other* people, who wanted me to give up a share of my credit, a portion of my money, a piece of my professional achievement, weren't my friends to begin with. Nor were they people I would ever really want, truth be told, to *be* my friends.

That's when I finally did what I should have done in the first place. I picked up the phone again and I called the Writers Guild.

The guild explained the process—how I had to lodge my objection to Sally's claim, what share of the story payment was at stake, and how I was to make my case for the arbitration panel to decide—in an entirely neutral fashion.

Once I had made up my mind to proceed with the arbitration—and I had—the most important thing I had to do was write a letter, laying out my understanding of what had happened, and why I thought I was entitled to the full and sole credit on the episode. Writing such a letter is optional, but you're crazy if you don't; the other side will. It seemed like it wouldn't be a particularly arduous task, but it did take longer than I'd expected.

Not because I was unsure of the facts—I knew how the whole affair had gone down—but because I had to keep my focus. I had to forget about the irrelevant stuff—the way I felt I was getting strong-armed into letting Sally share the story credit, for instance—and stick to the facts and only the facts. The assignment meeting. The outlines. The dates on which I'd submitted those outlines, the dates of the subsequent drafts of the script.

Once I'd finished writing the letter, I had to go back over it and carefully—surgically—remove the spleen. No matter how I felt about the producers' tactics or Sally's grab, there was no point in coming off as angry or accusatory. This letter would be read by three other writers, members of the guild, whose verdict would determine who got credit for what. And I suspected they wouldn't take kindly to one writer slinging mud at the other. My goal was to present myself as levelheaded, objective, and professional, while at the same time I was secretly hoping that Sally's letter would be all the things mine was not.

I had also been under the mistaken apprehension that it was up to me to gather all the relevant documents in the case—the outlines, the drafts of the script, any notes that I took, memos that I sent—and submit those to the arbitrators. But that's not so, and in retrospect, I can see why. It would be way too easy for a writer to go back after the fact and start producing notes or memoranda that subtly, or blatantly for that matter, bolstered his case.

Instead, it's up to the production company to gather up all these materials and send them off, in a great big box, to the guild. Then, as one of the writers who's a party to the arbitration, you'll receive a list of all the documents that have been submitted, and on which the credits decision is to be based. You're supposed to look this list over and make sure it's got everything it ought to have, at least from your point of view.

When I got mine, that's when I knew just how determined this network of friends was to get Sally what she wanted. At first, the list looked okay—long, in fact. Then, on second glance, I noticed a puzzling gap. My outlines were missing. It looked for all the world like the producers had come up with an idea, which Sally outlined for them, and which I then wrote. Based on this box of material, even I would have awarded her story credit.

When I called the production office to ask where my outlines were, I got stonewalled at first. The assistant, I was told, had gathered together and sent everything he could find in the producers' files.

So once again, I had to do what I should have done in the first place: I notified the guild of the problem, listed all of my outlines by date (fortunately, and take a lesson from this, I had kept copies of every one), and let the guild pursue it.

And guess what? Like Hillary Clinton's billing records, those outlines, miraculously, turned up. No one ever said how, or where, but they just showed up again, and were submitted to the arbitration panel.

Then I waited, though not exactly with bated breath. What would be, would be. I'd done what I could do, and more importantly, I'd done what I thought was the right thing. Even if I lost, I'd at least stood up for myself against that powerful cabal of friends.

In the end, I prevailed. As a party to the arbitration, you don't get the inside details, how the decision was reached or any of that, but I did get the notice that I had received a unanimous verdict. The sole and unsullied credit, for story and teleplay, was mine.

Not only that—I have actually worked for those same producers again since the arbitration. They offered me an assignment, and I accepted. (If you rule out working for unpleasant producers in this town, you might as well leave now.) But do I now keep a copy of every single thing I write for them? Do I make notes of every meeting I go to, and every instruction I receive? You bet. I do this, in fact, with every project I do, for whatever company at all. So should you.

And has Sally managed, as implied, to blackball me in the industry? No. I doubt, to be honest, she gave the whole thing more than a moment's thought. She went after the story credit because she thought she'd get no resistance. Has she invited me to a backyard barbecue? No.

But since that's about the only fallout I can see from this whole contretemps, I'd say it was all worth it in the end.

Part IX

Endgames

Bad Signs

■■■ I once had a literary agent, years ago, who said to me, "I don't know why anybody'd want to be a writer. It's like being fired your whole life."

At that moment, I didn't know exactly what he meant, but I learned. When you're a writer and you do a bad job on something, you're fired. When you're a writer and you do a good job, you're still fired. The project's over, and you've got to move on and find your next assignment.

Nowhere is this more true than in TV, where only one in a hundred shows goes the distance. If you're on staff, and the bubble bursts, you're out there, with a half dozen other writers, scrambling for your next post. But the failure of the show you were on is no blot on your professional record. Sure, it's nice to have been on a hit show, but having served time on a flop doesn't really do you any damage. I've met very successful, well-respected writers in this town whose résumés include half a dozen out-and-out disasters. What's most impressive to anyone who works in this business is that these writers have clearly been so highly regarded that they've consistently found work. That's a very laudable achievement.

Especially as so much of your career depends upon luck. Yes, you must have ability, as I've mentioned, but a bit of luck never hurt either. A case in point is two writers I know—we'll call them Jules and Jim—both of whom landed their first jobs on the staff of the same CBS show. When that show was canceled, Jules got a job on another show, which went on to become a big hit; Jim, unfortunately, got a job on a new show that was not a hit. Jules, ever since, has managed to surf from one successful show to another, while Jim—a writer who, trust me, has just as much talent as Jules—has drawn nothing but losers. Don't weep for Jim—he's still done fine. But I'm sure he would have liked a couple of the lucky breaks that just happened to go Jules's way.

Even if you're lucky enough to get a staff position on an unqualified hit, there's always the question of hanging on to it. Each season, new producers, new executives, new writers are brought on board, and in the game of musical chairs that follows, it's not always easy to cling to your own seat.

That's why every TV writer I know is always keeping his eyes and his ears open, trying to stay abreast of what's happening in the business, which shows are faltering, which ones are picking up steam, who's working where, what's coming down the pike. And in their spare time, even when they're on staff, they're updating their résumés, keeping clean copies within easy reach, and cranking out fresh spec scripts so that, if the worst should happen and they find themselves out in the marketplace again, their agents have some new material to advertise their services with.

I, of course, did none of these things, even when the signs were becoming unmistakably clear, to everyone but me, that my tenure at *Dark World* was coming to a close.

There was, for instance, the Christmas party incident. I was sitting in the office of the executive producer, Carl, one morning when he happened to mention something about the company party that night.

Company party? I looked blank.

"I'll give you the book at the party," he reiterated, then said, "You're coming, aren't you?"

"I don't know," I said. "I wasn't invited."

This set off a flurry of phone calls and apologies and excuses ("Of course you're invited—you're the story editor!") and that afternoon a copy of the official invitation was faxed to my home office. My wife was so embarrassed that she said she didn't want to go. I thought, *Well, maybe it was just an oversight, or the invitation got lost in the mail. We have to go.*

Then I found out that Bill, the other writer in the L.A. office, had also just been faxed a last-minute invitation. Bill and I had a phone powwow. "Maybe the party was just for the network execs and the advertisers—the big guys, that sort of thing," Bill suggested.

"Or maybe it was more for the office support staff—you know, the secretaries and assistants and copy-room guys," I threw in.

"Yeah, that could be," Bill said.

Whatever the reason, we decided to overlook the slight and go to the party, which was being held on a big boat in Newport Beach. My wife, who still thought we should have shown enough self-respect to decline, reluctantly agreed to come along, as did Bill's partner, Pam. And, of course, because I was so concerned about missing the boat's departure time, we were among the very first guests to cross the gangplank and go aboard.

The first person I saw was one of the top studio executives. "Maybe you were right," I said to Bill under my breath. "Maybe the party *was* only for the big shots and sponsors."

The second person we saw was the guy who picked up our lunches and brought them to the office. "Maybe not," Bill said.

As the boat filled up with other guests—anybody and everybody even remotely affiliated with the show, including people I couldn't even identify—Bill and I stood by the railing, sipping our drinks and wondering just how all of these invitations had arrived safe and sound while ours, and ours alone, had gone astray. My wife was still so mortified she wanted to jump ship before we pulled away from the dock, but by now I was determined to stick it out and have a good time, no matter how unwanted we were.

You can imagine how successful that was.

• • •

Still, I didn't get it. The missing invitation was only the first sign of my impending doom.

The second was my missing computer. One day, I came into the office, and the laptop, which the show had generously provided for me, was gone.

What was worse, and stranger, was that nobody seemed very concerned. A two-thousand-dollar machine had been stolen from my unlocked office (our offices *had* no locks on them, a problem I had complained about earlier) and nobody at the show, from the producers to the office manager, whom I had immediately alerted to the loss, seemed overly troubled about the loss this would incur to my productivity. True, locks were installed on our office doors a week later, but the missing computer was never found . . . or, more tellingly, replaced.

By now, even I was beginning to feel the shift in the winds. Was I no longer . . . indispensable?

Clue number three was coming.

I came into the office one morning, armed with the legal pads on which I now wrote when I was at work, and found that Matt, my assistant, was sitting at my desk.

Or what used to be my desk.

In order to make room for the staff of a new show they were simultaneously producing, the company had moved Matt into my office. Fortunately, he had brought along his own chair.

Matt and I had a pretty good time over the next few days, redecorating, eating in, trying out our movie pitches on each other.

It only got crowded when, a week after that, Bill was moved in, too.

The next step was inevitable. One day, Carl called me into his office and told me that if I wanted to, I could work from home from now on. And so could Bill, he said, for that matter.

I won't deny that, apart from the obvious demotion, there was something not altogether displeasing about this prospect. I could stay home? Not set an alarm? Not drive to work every day? Maybe even go to a movie matinee, with no one being the wiser?

The following Monday, I came in to the office and packed my stuff into a couple of banker's boxes. I shook hands with Matt, left him my keys to the office, and, as I carried the boxes into the hall, Matt cupped his hands to his mouth and called out for all to hear, "Dead man walking!"

A reverent hush fell over everyone as I passed.

About three weeks later, I noticed that my salary checks had stopped coming. A call to my agent, who in turn called the producers, revealed that my services had been curtailed. No one from the show had bothered to call and tell me. When the season officially wrapped, I received in the mail a *Dark World* penknife.

Heaven, Hell, and Purgatory

■ ■ ■ There are essentially two modes of being for a TV writer—on staff or out there hustling.

When you're on staff, you spend a lot of time fantasizing about the freelance life. Every time you have to attend another pointless and interminable meeting, you dream of the days when your time was your own. Every time you have to kowtow to another executive producer, or pay respectful attention to his mindless blather, you think of being your own boss again, writing what you want, on your own schedule.

Then, of course, it happens. Your contract's not renewed or the show's canceled, and suddenly you're back where you started, scrambling for your next job, dreaming of those halcyon days when you drew a weekly paycheck, when you had a cozy little office to go to, other writers to fraternize with, and you knew what to say when people at parties asked you where you worked.

At bottom, the life of the writer is one of constant longing for whatever you don't have, until you have it, when you can start longing for what you just lost.

God, we're a miserable lot. No wonder nobody wants to live with us.

For a fortunate few, there is a way station of sorts, a sort of purgatory, somewhere between the poles of employment and poverty. It isn't heaven, and it isn't hell (though it is often so characterized). It is, in fact, a no-man's-land from which you may emerge victorious or where you may languish unnoticed and alone. It all depends on what you do with it.

It's called . . . a development deal. And it's the ultimate test of what you've got.

Let's say you've just come off of working on staff at a successful show, and as a result you're still carrying some of that heat. The studios think you know something; they think you were in some way responsible for that hit you were working on (and they may even be right). Sure, they'd like to have you writing for one of their other shows, but if they haven't got a spot right now, or if they think you've really got the juice, they may opt to set you up on your own, and see if you can't come up with the next big, fresh, original (but not *too* original) hit show.

Although I've heard several friends, who've had them, complain about development deals, if you ask me they're the ultimate plum. My friend Joseph had a couple of rooms, with sofas, chairs, and a mini fridge, on the top floor of a building on a studio lot. There, he lay around all day, spinning out airy conceits, in one week racking out six short pilot ideas. He invited me up to read them. And let me tell you, they were the most nonsensical things I'd ever read. I had a suspicion that Joseph knew that, too. After I'd mumbled some vaguely complimentary remarks, he waved it all off and said, "So it's garbage, what do I care? I've just got to show them that I'm doing something for the money."

"But why not do something that you really like?"

"They wouldn't buy it even if I did."

It never fails to astonish me, but what the studios, despite all their dough and all their resources, seem to have missed is one simple truth about the writing trade: There are caretakers, and there are creators, and very seldom do you find a writer who's both.

Joseph was a caretaker. He'd worked on two or three hit

shows, he'd written solid episodes for all of them, he'd carried out his assigned missions with alacrity and aplomb, but he didn't have any ideas of his own. Maybe at some time in his life, before he'd burned out on all the other shows, he'd had something to say, some stories of his own that he wanted to tell, but he didn't have them now. He'd lost that spark. All he could do now was take orders and deliver the goods. You could rely on him always to do a more than competent job, but you couldn't expect him to come up with something on his own.

I've had other friends who were *made* for development deals. They're the creators, the kind of people who could come up with a handful of high concepts over lunch, more ideas than you could even absorb and process. But they're not necessarily the people whom you'd trust to develop and run a show each week.

My friend Wendy, for instance, was like a pinwheel, throwing off ideas right and left, but the weird thing was, she couldn't tell the difference between the good ones and the bad ones. She was already onto the next big notion. Fortunately, she had people around her who *could* tell the difference, and when one of these ideas in particular appeared to be really working, her friendly advisors got her to buckle down and concentrate on that one notion long enough for it to take shape, take wing, and become a reasonably successful show (now in its third season).

Since then, Wendy, who was always more interested in the life of the mind than the tube, in ideas rather than rating shares, has taken her regular "created by" checks, and her mounting residuals, and gone off to teach at an Eastern college, where she fits in much better than she ever did in TV.

Most development deals run for a year or two; the friends of mine who have had them have been paid well into the six, or even seven, figures. One friend has had two of these deals, each one lasting for two years, and both times he spent the first year writing pilots that nobody wanted, and the second year—after the studio paying him had decided that they wanted *something* to show for their money—running one of their other shows. Sure, he would have liked to have "created" something, a show of his own, but in the past year alone, he's made close to a million dollars (maybe more, he doesn't tell me everything) shepherding a preexisting property through one more semisuccessful season. He's no longer expected to create a hit, he's just expected not to kill one.

Two for the Load

■ ■ ■ Maybe it's because writing for TV is such a chancy profession—one day you're sitting in your plush "development deal" office, the next you're sitting home in the middle of the day, watching *The Young and the Restless*—that so many writers decide at one point or another to pair off. I've done all kinds of writing, but I've never known any other area of the profession where the urge to team up was stronger or more common than it is in TV. In fact, if I go through a mental catalogue of all my friends in the TV writing trade, I can't come up with one—not one—who isn't now, or wasn't once, a member of a writing team. In many ways, the business lends itself to it.

The moment that two TV writers decide to work together, they have just doubled their contacts. It's as if their Rolodexes had just seamlessly meshed, and each writer can now comb through the other's, looking for people they've always wanted to reach, executives for whom they have long had a project that might work, connections that suddenly spur them on to some new and possibly salable thought. I once collaborated on a project with a friend whose own friend had just been put in charge of finding "cutting-edge, innovative, non-network kinds of ideas" for a major network. (This, by the way, is what all the major networks always claim to be looking for, even though they aren't.) Anyway, my friend and I quickly hatched an idea that sounded cutting-edge without really *being* cutting-edge, that looked innovative but wasn't, that pretended to be off-road but was in fact perfectly suitable for a major network run, and submitted it to my friend's friend's office. Then we waited five or six weeks, cooling our overheated jets, before reading in the trades that his friend had just been demoted to a job in distribution.

Okay, so it doesn't always work, but in this business, it's all about taking any shot you can.

Collaborating can also give a jump-start to your backlog of stalled ideas or half-completed concepts. Every writer has a batch of these—ideas that never quite went anywhere, scripts that got started and then ground to a halt, treatments that never went beyond a few pages of random noodlings. (I'd have to rent a storage locker to house mine at this point.) But once you have a partner in crime, you can haul these half-formed creatures out into the light ("Look, I call this one Bruno—don't you think he'd make a great animated sitcom idea?") and see what your partner thinks. He may not agree with you or see all the virtues in Bruno that you do, but for once you're getting an opinion untainted by any other agenda. He's not worrying about the network schedule or his own chance of scoring the next episode; all he's thinking about is whether or not the two of you can spruce this thing up and sell it for a lot of money. From which he will take half.

Do not be disappointed, however, if your partner doesn't think you can sell it. I've worked with a couple of writing partners over the years, and both times that we showed each other our secret children, nothing much came of it. No formal adoptions were made. With one collaborator, we kind of knocked around an old idea I'd had, banged out a treatment, and then left it at that. With another, we took an old feature script of his, lifted the core idea, then tried to fashion a series out of it. I think, in both instances, the attempts were made more out of politeness than genuine conviction, but they still served a purpose.

Taking these shots got us working in harness together; it allowed each of us to see what kind of ideas the other one was most excited about. We could see not only where our interests dovetailed, but where they diverged, and it gave us a much better notion of what each of us was planning to bring to the table.

Then the hard part began—coming up with a new idea that we'd built, as partners, from the ground up.

Although most of this process looks suspiciously like playtime rather than work, work is what it is. Sure, you may be sitting around the coffeehouse, your spoons resting on the legal pad, but what you're really doing is exploring, in a casual, caffeine-enriched setting, a range of ideas. You're free-associating. This can also be done while walking on the beach, throwing a Frisbee back and forth, or chatting on the phone late at night. (Night conversations are better than daytime ones because there's less chance of getting interrupted by those constant call-waiting clicks.) Go to the Brentwood Country Mart, the Farmers Market, or Jerry's Deli in Westwood, any day of the week, and you'll see writing teams lingering over bowls of soup, slices of pie, or fruit smoothies as they wonder how to open up their story, strip-mine a comic vein, or get their agents to return their calls.

But somewhere in all this banter, debate, and kvetching, an idea eventually struggles upward and moves toward the light . . . an idea that both partners feel they've had a hand in creating, an idea that excites them both to the point where they're actually willing to leave the beach or the restaurant, go to their workspace, and settle down to some serious writing.

That's where the really thorny problems crop up.

Who lies on the sofa, and who sits at the computer? Who pins notecards to the bulletin board, and who paces the room tossing a Nerf ball against the walls? Who wants to work from eight A.M. to noon, and who wants to start at noon and work till five? I'd bet that far more partnerships have broken up over logistical questions than creative ones. When I was working with a guy named Chuck, I would wake up in the morning, around the crack of ten o'clock, and find an endless scroll of fax pages snaking across my office floor. Chuck had been up since daybreak, feverishly writing. Over coffee and a bagel, I'd read over the pages, make my notes, and when we got together that afternoon, we'd discuss the changes and what had to be done next. That night, around eight o'clock, I'd sit down at my computer and I'd write till sometime past midnight. Before turning in, I'd fax the pages to Chuck's house, and he'd read them when he got up with the dawn's early light. A system like that might not work for everyone, but for us it did. We didn't plan it that way, it just evolved, from our own natural biorhythms.

Most writing partners don't much care how or when the other writer writes, just so long as the writing gets done and the burden is shared. Sometimes one of you is better at conceptualizing, at seeing the big picture, than getting the day-to-day pages done. Or one of you does better dialogue than the other. Or one does the heavy-lifting of structure, while the other peppers the scenes with laugh-lines. No two writers are alike, no two writers have the exact same strengths, and if they did, what would be the point of collaborating?

With Chuck I could depend upon him to turn out more pages of rough script than a whole battalion of staff writers, and he could count on me to throw out some of it but find the great stuff that was buried in there—and there was always great stuff—and polish it up till it shone.

In the case of another guy I collaborated with, Phil, the relationship broke down over perfectionism—his, not mine—although if you asked Phil, he'd probably tell you that things fell apart because I was too hasty and market-driven. There may be two sides to every story, but since this is my book and not Phil's, I'm going to say that the problem lay with Phil's congenital inability to let go of anything. He did brilliant work, which is why I teamed up with him in the first place, but what I didn't know was that he could never stop tinkering with something. No matter how good it was, or how long we'd already worked on it, it was never quite ready to be shown, it always needed just a little more work, there was always some problem that ought to be looked at just one more time.

In a desperate attempt to break one of these logjams, Phil and I went up to Lake Arrowhead, where he had the use of a cousin's empty cabin. Phil went out on the deck with his laptop, and I stayed upstairs, working on mine. And at the end of each day, I'd have several pages to show—not flawless, but pretty well done—and Phil would have four lines. The lines were good, I'm not saying they weren't, but at that rate, we'd have a one-hour script done in about sixteen years. Phil hated it when I pushed him to work just a teensy bit faster, and I wasn't crazy about it when he'd start nitpicking at every scene I'd written.

Clearly, though we'd been close friends since college, this was not a collaboration with a bright future. When we came back from the cabin, we decided to go our separate ways, me to pursue my own brilliant career, and Phil to pursue his. Interestingly enough, Phil stopped trying to make a living as a writer per se about a year later; he took a job, instead, as a script reader, where he wrote incisive "coverage" (summaries and critiques) on spec scripts that had been submitted to the studio. Not surprisingly, as his instincts and talents were primarily analytical, he flourished, and today he heads up a fairly sizable story department.

Even if things don't always work out in collaborations, the advantages are so apparent, and in some cases so tangible (ask Lowell Ganz and Babaloo Mandel), that working in teams is never going to go out of style. For one thing, and this is undoubtedly the chief impetus, Hollywood can be hard, *very* hard, on the ego. For every yes you get, there are a hundred no's. For every call of yours that gets returned, a dozen don't. For every meeting you take, three get canceled at the last minute. When things are going badly, when the world is too much, it can be an absolute lifesaver to have someone else, your partner, in the very same boat. Some of the best laughs I've had, times when I've completely lost it and doubled over, speechless with laughter, have been the times when a partner and I have undergone some particularly debilitating experience together—a gruesome pitch meeting where everything went wrong, a notes session where neither one of us could follow what was being said, a surreal communiqué from a studio savant. Once, when Chuck and I were leaving a studio lot where our ideas had not been, shall we say, welcomed, the gate guard inexplicably motioned us to the side of the drive, motioned for us to get out of the vehicle, then methodically searched the car. Chuck and I stood there helplessly while he popped my trunk and combed through my beach blankets, cooler, emergency dog food rations, bottled water, Gordon Lightfoot tapes (that's what embarrassed me the most), searching for . . . what?

"Is there anything in particular you're looking for?" I timidly asked.

The guard, who looked like Ving Rhames after he'd just stubbed his toe, slammed the trunk down and glared at me. "Studio property."

"Ah," Chuck said. "We thought it was just because our ideas stunk so bad."

"If it was that," the guard said, "I'd be searching cars like this all day long."

Moments in our career that will live forever.

Having a partner around can also give you that backup you occasionally need. In pitch meetings, when I've started to flag or I don't seem to be getting the point across ("This is *funny*, you oafs, can't you see that!?") it's good to have a partner who can step in and take over for a few minutes. "What Robert was trying to say, until he temporarily took leave of his senses, was that we see this script as a comedy." He can try to bring the room around again to a friendlier, more receptive mood.

With your partner there, you're also not so outnumbered by the staff and studio people. You're not the only one sweating in the pitch chair; there's another guy sweating beside you. And in the postmortem, you have another witness with whom you can confer.

"Did he really say that we should tell the whole story from the point of view of the hamster?"

"No, not exactly. He only said that we should make sure we build in a deep emotional conflict for the hamster. That's all."

"Oh. Whew."

Finally when you sit down to translate all these notes, suggestions, and directives into an actual script, there are two of you to make sure you stay on course. Whenever you're overcome by the impulse to throw over the traces and do something the *right* way, no matter what the consequences, your partner is there to remind you what the network wants, or what the producers said, or why the hamster *must* be brought forward in the story. In a good collaboration, you alternately don, and doff, the hat of reason.

When good collaborations go bad, they go bad for a lot of reasons, but part of the problem is simply built in. The reason writers become writers, in large measure, is that they want to do what they want to do, to say what they want to say, the way they want to say it. Even in the best collaborations, compromise is a daily event. When you're writing the script together, you must give in on certain things—lines you don't much like, scenes you'd rather do without—simply because your partner feels strongly about them, and he wants them in. And he's going to have to do the same for you.

Ideally, when the script is finished, you'll both be proud of it, but I'd be lying to you if I didn't admit that, in my heart of hearts, I've never been 100 percent satisfied with a script I've collaborated on. (Of course, I've never been one hundred percent satisfied with anything I've ever done, but that's another issue.) On every script I've written with a partner, there are parts of it that still make me want to throw myself back at the keyboard and do a fast and furious rewrite. For instance, there's the flatulence joke in the action-thriller that I could not persuade my partner to delete; there's the "camel bit" in a one-hour drama. And I'm sure there are elements I put into those same scripts that my collaborators would love to get rid of (over my dead body).

There's another factor that comes into play, too. Not only do writers like to do things their own way, they are also uncomfortable telling someone else what to do. Most writers have opted for this precarious career in part because they don't want to be part of a big corporate structure, they don't want to be an employee anywhere . . . but they also don't want to be anybody's boss. They're as uninterested in pushing someone around as they are in being pushed around. If business is a competition, writers have chosen not to compete, except with themselves. They're interested in what they can create on their own, and how well they can create it, and the critic they most want to please, impossible as it may be, is their internal one. A veteran

TV writer once announced at an event I attended, "I've never written a word that I'm not proud of!" and I remember thinking, even though I hardly knew the guy, that he must be a total hack. Not to mention an egotistical one. I've never met what I would regard as a *real* writer, who isn't forever wishing that his work couldn't have gone just a little bit better, that he could not have come just a bit closer to realizing on paper that story, that voice, that vision, that feeling that had compelled him to sit down and try to capture it in the first place.

And that, in a long-winded way, is why a lot of collaborators ultimately decide to go back to doing things their own solitary fashion.

On a practical note, the one inescapable *dis*advantage of collaborating is that the work you've done together, whether it was a commissioned episode of something or a spec script, is fairly useless to each of you individually. If the title page has got two names on it, neither one of you can lay full claim to the work and show it as a sample. If you sell it, fine, then you just split the money as you had always planned. But if you were planning to use this script as a means of rustling up other work or assignments just for yourself, don't bother. It's ethically a little suspect, and professionally unhelpful.

Nor do you need such a transgression to stimulate any ill feeling between you and your erstwhile partner; there's usually plenty of ill will already. When writing teams break up, it's like a marriage dissolving; and just as in a divorce, the two partners often go on to a lifetime of bitter enmity. You will seldom meet two people in Hollywood who hate each other with the heat, the vigor, the violence of ex-writing partners. I was once at a picnic in a local park, at which two ex-partners, neither one expecting to see the other, showed up. It was if Hamilton had just stumbled upon Burr. During what was supposed to be a friendly game of badminton, one of them thwapped the birdie so hard it left a dent in his ex-partner's forehead. The ex-partner threw his racquet, and before a punch could be thrown in return, several of us had to intervene.

Even though the birdie-swatter gathered up his thermos, his blanket, and his chicken salad and left, the picnic never quite recovered its air of innocence and fun.

Hired Guns

At the time I'm writing this, a sea change is occurring in the way that TV writers do business, and it's going to be awhile, maybe years, before we see how it all gets sorted out, but the opening shots have been fired, and the various factions are maneuvering for position.

It began, as do so many things in Hollywood, with a collective disgruntlement among the writers.

What with?

Our agents, what else.

But it wasn't until I was having dinner one night, at an expensive Italian restaurant, that I realized just how the ground was shifting.

I was dining with a couple of screenwriter friends, and complaining, as writers are wont to do, about my lack of work. At that point, my professional dry spell had lasted four months, and as a result I was desperately scanning the restaurant menu for an entrée under eighteen dollars. My friends told me they'd weathered some bad times, too, but ever since hiring their manager, their "quote" (the asking price for their work) had doubled and their workload had increased mightily.

"A manager?" I asked. "When did you get a manager?"

"Last year. And it's the best thing we ever did."

Up until that moment, I'd never even considered such a thing. Managers, I'd thought, were just for actors and singers and people like that; if writers used them at all, I figured, it was only the ones whose careers were so huge and lucrative, who had so many studios vying for their services, that they needed the extra layer of management simply to sort through all their offers.

But my two dinner friends were not in that category. Not by a long shot. And now, *they* had a manager?

I filed it away, until I happened to be sitting in the office of a TV writer friend, told her the story, and she said, "Me too. I've got a manager."

"You do?" Karen made a very nice living, but she was still just a staff story editor.

"Yes. I hired him about six months ago."

"And?"

"And he's gotten me a pilot commitment and a movie-of-the-week offer. I don't like paying the extra ten percent, on top of what I pay to my agent, but it's worth it overall. I'm still making more money than I ever used to."

I promptly added this to my burgeoning mental file, which just about exploded a week later when I had lunch with a guy who writes mystery movies for cable. Ted was a long-standing client at one of the big three agencies, but despite that, he still wasn't getting any work.

"And every time I complained, even a little, to my agent," he said, "he'd say something like, 'Don't worry about it—we'll get right on it.' "

"And would he?" I asked.

"I thought so," Ted said. "I'd get a call a few days later, and he'd have set up meetings for me with places all over town. And I'd go to the meetings, and I'd meet the producers or whoever, and I'd pitch some ideas, and then nothing would happen. I'd never actually get any work, and I was starting to get desperate."

That's when he decided to call a manager, whose name he'd been given by a friend. "And I was very reluctant to do it," Ted said. "I really thought the last thing I needed was another level of bureaucracy in my life—and another guy to pay out of whatever work I ever did find." But he made the call; he told the manager what was happening, and then the manager asked Ted to do something for him. He asked Ted to make up a list of all these appointments that his agency had set up for him over the last six months, and bring it to lunch the next day.

"I just figured he wanted to know where I'd already been," Ted said, so he dutifully wrote up the list and brought it with him.

Over lunch, the manager said, "Take out the list, but don't show it to me."

Ted did.

"Now," the manager said, "I'm going to tell you who's on the list. Check them off as I go."

To Ted's astonishment, the manager then proceeded to rattle off almost every name on the list. "How'd I do?" the manager asked.

"Very well," Ted said. "Almost a perfect score. But how did you do that?"

"Simple," the manager replied. "Those are all companies and producers that your agency represents or has some kind of deal going with. When you complain to the agency, and they don't know what to do for you, they set up these meaningless meetings so you'll get the impression that they're working for you. But they're not really. They're just spinning your wheels."

As Ted tells it, it was like a lightbulb going off in his head. That was certainly how it had felt. In meeting after meeting, he'd had the feeling it was just some sort of meet-and-greet, that nothing in the way of work was seriously available or even on the table, but he'd always put it down to his own paranoia and increasing desperation. He'd even begun to feel that it was his fault he wasn't getting any work out of these meetings, that he must be doing something wrong.

As he went on with his story, I sat there, dumbfounded, with my own lightbulb going off. Because that was exactly how I'd often felt about my own agents. Routinely, nothing would happen until I dared to raise my voice—enough to tell them I was starving—and then I'd get a meeting or two, with a development executive or a production company, but there was always some impediment to my actually getting any *work* from any of them. The show hadn't been picked up yet, the staff had no openings right then, the show was on hiatus, the producers were only hiring writers under five-foot-eight. No matter how reasonable, or unreasonable, there was always something that spelled, "No work, but thanks for coming in." And I, too, felt like I was somehow botching it time and again; I was always vaguely embarrassed to call my agent afterward, to thank him for setting up the meeting, but also to tell him nothing had come of it.

Ted's story made immediate and total sense to me, and when he finished by saying that his work had increased "by about four hundred percent" since taking on the manager, I decided I would be crazy not to give it a shot myself.

As a matter of professional etiquette, I didn't want to call Ted's manager. But I had a line on one myself, through my wife: Laurie liked to hike with a woman named Connie on Sunday mornings, and Connie's husband, Irv, happened to be a manager.

The one thing I knew for sure about this guy was that he must be doing something right. We'd gone to a party one night at his house, a beautiful spread up in Bel Air, where the chef from one of the best restaurants in town had been there personally to prepare the dinner, which the guests then enjoyed under umbrella-covered tables arranged around the large and sparkling pool. Irv had been very pleasant and welcoming, even showing me around the pool/guest house, but I can't say I was really at my ease. Irv was one of those guys who makes me feel like I'm not really a grown-up. He's tough, in a manly sort of way that I'll never be—square jaw, dark hair, unafraid to speak his mind. My jaw is soft, my hair is thin, and I'd much rather say whatever I think the other party would like to hear. Anything, basically, to avoid discomfort or conflict.

So even calling him up was for me a big and daring step. But the alternative—slow starvation by way of EGO—looked even bleaker. When I got him on the phone, I asked if he even represented writers ("Sure I do—didn't you meet some of them at the party?") and we arranged to have lunch the next day at a popular restaurant on the Sunset Strip.

There, Irv told me a little about himself: the fact that he'd worked at a big agency for many years; before that he'd worked for his family for a while, collecting money for their plumbing supply business in the Midwest. One day, he told me, while he was collecting a debt in a particularly rough part of town, he had returned to his car to find several gang members standing around it, and one of them, blocking the driver's-side door, was holding a baseball bat in his hand.

"So what did you do?" I asked.

Irv shrugged and took a forkful of his salad. "I took out my gun and I put it in his mouth."

"You had a gun?"

"You wouldn't set foot in that neighborhood without one."

"And it was loaded?"

"What good would it do if it wasn't?" He looked at me as if he'd never seen such a wuss in his life.

I looked back at him, thinking, *A gangster . . . I'm about to hire a gangster.*

Then he went on to explain to me what a manager can and can't do. He can guide your career, he can help you focus your efforts, make choices, direct yourself.

"But can you, I mean could you, I mean would you," I stammered, "do you think you'd be able to help me, for instance, find work?"

"Managers by law are not allowed to procure employment for their clients."

This was my first stunning surprise.

"Well, then, could you, if I found some work, help me maybe to negotiate the deal, so that I could get more money, or more work, out of it?"

"No. Managers by law can't negotiate on behalf of their clients. That's for the agents to do."

"So, I'd still have to keep my agent?"

"Yes."

"And pay him, and—not that I'm sure it wouldn't be worth it—pay you, too?"

"Yes."

While it seemed mind-boggling at first, what Irv had just told me was the truth. Managers cannot, by law, procure employment or negotiate deals for their clients. So what good was Irv going to do me, I thought? Why were all these people recommending I get a manager? What was the point, if a manager couldn't get you jobs or money?

I was wondering about all this as we left the restaurant. Irv took a call on his cell phone, barked "No! Tell the studio we've got a deal and that's it!"—then stopped beside a gleaming Jaguar convertible clearly parked in a red no-parking zone a few yards from the door to the restaurant. I had parked my own car three blocks away, in the first spot I could find.

"Geez," I said, "it looks like you parked in a no-parking zone."

Again, he looked at me like he couldn't figure out how I'd managed to live this long. "It's where the shade is," he explained, while raising the hand with the cell phone toward the tree branches hanging overhead.

Of course. It's where the shade is. I thought about that as I hurried back to my own car, blazing in the sun at a meter where the time had just run out.

At home, I agonized over the whole business with my wife. I told her about the gun-in-the-mouth story.

She said his wife Connie was very nice.

I said he'd put a gun in a man's mouth.

She said, "What else has he done?"

I replied that he'd been a VP at a big agency for many years.

"There," Laurie said, "he knows what he's doing. Hire him."

I made one last call before deciding. I spoke to my father in Florida, told him the whole story. He said, "You're my son, and I love you, but that's what you need."

"What?"

"Somebody to put a gun in their mouth."

• • •

As Irv had explained to me over lunch, the normal commitment to a manager is two years. A year at least. So once I called him back and said, in effect, let's do it, I knew I was on the hook for a while. Which, of course, immediately threw me into a panic of self-doubt and second-guessing. Who was *I* to have a manager? What did I have to *manage*? If I got even less work than I had at present, what would I do next—bring in a board of directors?

Irv told me to come by his office and pick up some scripts he wanted me to read, from a show where one of his clients was already placed. His offices turned out to be on the second floor of an unprepossessing building on Melrose. Brown carpeting, musty halls, rows of identical closed doors with tarnished name plates that said things like "Global Entertainment, Inc.," "Stars of Tomorrow, International," "Tip-Top Talent." With every step I took, I felt more and more like Barton Fink.

Irv's offices were marginally better, but not much. At least he had the suite at the end of the hall. "I don't believe in spending a lot of money on offices," Irv said when I popped my head in. He was squashed behind a butcher-block table in a small room whose walls were plastered with movie and theater posters. His assistant handed me a box of material, Irv took another phone call—the red lights on his phone console were flashing like a theater marquee—and I left.

Now, I felt, I was really in for it.

One week later, I was arriving at Universal Studios to pitch to the show where Irv had a client on staff. To my own surprise, I felt, almost from the moment I sat down, that the atmosphere in the room was somehow different—better—than I was used to. When EGO had set up meetings, everything had always been cordial, but there was never a clear sense of purpose. (I was reminded of what Ted's manager had told him, about the pointless appointments.) At those meetings, we'd make small talk until the talk was absolutely tiny, then mosey around to the ostensible purpose of my visit—*work*—then we'd mosey right on past it again, and before you can say "Validate your parking?" I was out in the parking lot again, clutching my stub with the one-hour stamp on it.

Not this time. In this meeting, there were the usual preliminaries—*Can we get you something to drink? How about those Dodgers? We liked your sample scripts*—but then the show-runner (Irv's client) said, "So, what have you got for us today?" and the mood in the room immediately became more serious, almost as if—and this was so strange for me—we were actually there *to do business*.

Was this, I wondered, what it was like for successful writers? You went to meetings where they were actually prepared to assign you some work?

I launched into my first pitch, and within minutes I knew that the room was with me. Two staff writers, who were also in attendance, were taking copious notes as I spoke, and the show-runner was nodding approvingly.

Oh, and I should probably mention, there was one other thing working for me in the room.

One of those two staff writers was a guy who had pitched to *me*—successfully—when I was story editor at another show. I wasn't sure if I should bring this up when I got there, but the moment we'd assembled in the room, the writer had said, "I don't know if you remember me" (which, of course, I did) "but you were so generous to me when I came in to pitch to you last year. And I wanted to thank you again for all your help."

I said something suitably humble and self-effacing, but silently I prayed he would know that *now* would be the perfect time to return the favor.

He did, thereby proving that TV karma can exist.

The whole meeting went very well, and I left with one assignment firmly in hand and another one in the offing.

That night, my wife and I were scheduled to see Irv at a nightclub, where one of his comedy clients was performing. When we walked in, Irv strolled over from the bar and said, "So, how'd it go?"

"I got an assignment," I said proudly.

To which he replied by taking my cheek between his thumb and forefinger . . . and pinching it.

After we were shown to our table, my wife laughed and said, "He pinched your cheek!"

"Sure. I got the job. But what happens next time, if I don't? Next time, he might put a gun in my mouth."

Laurie put a reassuring hand on my arm. "I don't think he'd do that."

And frankly, I knew he wouldn't either. But I liked the gag too much to let it go.

Do agents mind when their clients hire managers?

That's an interesting question.

You would think they'd be happy about it. After all, there's now another person out there beating the bushes, trying to uncover opportunities to move the client's career along. And if the manager succeeds, and *finds* something, the agent—with no effort whatsoever—will be able to commission the work at his usual 10 percent, anyway.

But it doesn't always go that smoothly. Agents, I have learned, feel threatened by managers. Put down. Dissed. When I told my agent I was hiring Irv, the first words out of his mouth were, "You're hiring Irv?"

"You know him?"

"Mm-hm." Long pause. "But isn't he a little *Old* Hollywood?"

He said it as if Irv, a middle-aged man, had worked with Cecil B. DeMille and Lillian Gish.

"I don't know," I said. "He returns my calls, he tells the truth, he reads my scripts. Is that what you'd call Old Hollywood?"

The agent decided to try another tack. "But do you really want to give away another ten or fifteen percent of your income?"

"No, not really." That much I had to confess. "But since at present I don't have any income, I can take the hit."

The next time my agent brought the matter up—"So, how's that manager of yours working out?"—it was a couple of weeks later, and I was able to say, with some satisfaction, "Oh, haven't you received the call yet?"

"What call?"

"The call from the show where I just sold a story. The show that Irv got me into."

There was an awkward silence on the line, which got even more awkward when I told the agent the name of the show.

Without so much as a hint of shame, the agent said, "I've got a client that I've been killing myself to get in there all season. Who did you meet with? Who can I call over there?"

I actually held the phone away from my face and stared at it. This was surreal. My agent was telling me he'd been trying desperately to place some *other* client at this show—and not me—and now he wanted to use *my* connection to try it again?

"Why don't we just concentrate for now," I said, "on wrapping up the paperwork on my deal? Then we'll see how I can help you out with your other clients."

The fundamental reason that many writers now have a manager, in addition to an agent, is that managers have in many respects taken over the duties that agents abrogated long ago. Even though managers are technically not allowed to procure the jobs, or negotiate the fees, most of them in effect do just that, though they cannot admit to doing so. I don't want to get Irv into any trouble, so I will state for the record that he does not perform either of those tasks, but I will say this: After eight weeks of working with a manager, I had on my desk more work than agents had placed there in years.

What writers have to recognize is that agencies have many writers on their roster, and when a position or a job comes up, all of the agents at the agency are alerting their own clients to the opportunity and sending them over to pitch. Your very *own* agent may be sending three or four other writers besides you, and it doesn't really matter to him whether you get it or one of his other clients does. He gets his commission no matter what.

A manager, on the other hand, will be less open-minded. He's got all his chips riding on you and you alone, and consequently he will want to make sure that *you're* the one who lands the gig.

Managers can also badger your agent in ways that you would

never dare. There's nothing most writers hate more than having to place those pleading calls to their agents, to find out if, by any chance, the agent has found the time to do something on their behalf. But managers thrive on such stuff. In my experience, managers are, by their very nature, aggressive and without shame. (Are they the next stage in the natural evolution of agents? Perhaps the scientific establishment should take a look at this.)

Managers will call an agent ten times if that's what it takes to get him on the line. And since the manager's income also depends on the agent closing some deals, the manager has a very strong, built-in incentive to beat the agent about the ears (something you may dream about, but never actually get to do). I know for a fact that my agents dread hearing that Irv is on the line, and it never fails to give me pleasure.

Recently, an old novel I wrote was optioned by a big company, with an eye toward turning it into a one-hour series. A conference call was arranged, and on separate lines we had a couple of agents, a couple of producers (who had once owed me $7,500, a sum that the agency—which also represented the producers—had persuaded me not to nag them about actually paying me), and Irv; in no time at all, the negotiations had turned prickly. "I'm just here to protect Robert's interests," Irv kept saying, which only got the agency delegation—who were, after all, my agents—that much more irritated.

"We're looking out for Robert's interests in this deal, too," one of them replied acidly.

"Maybe," Irv said. "What I see you protecting is your packaging fee. You are getting one on this deal, aren't you?"

"Possibly," the agent answered.

"That's good, because if you do, then Robert won't have to pay any agency commission."

A fact that until that moment I had not been aware of.

"The deal isn't finalized yet," the agent said. "We'll have to see how it plays out."

Among the points that still had to be discussed was what percentage of the AGR I would receive. The figure was at 2½ percent, and at some point everyone else on the line fell silent and

I realized that they were all waiting for me to agree, or disagree, with that number. I felt the way I used to feel in orchestra practice, when a solo for the French horn (my instrument) came up. Since I never could follow the music, I was used to playing whenever the trumpets did, and resting whenever they rested. But every once in a while the trumpets would stop, I'd stop too, and I'd suddenly realize that Mrs. Garrett, the conductor, was banging her stick on the music stand and glaring at me.

"French horn solo, Mr. Masello!"

That was exactly how it felt when the conversation stopped just now and everyone waited impatiently for me to give my okay on the AGR. "Two and a half percent, did you say?" I didn't want to look like a pushover. "Well, I was thinking more along the lines of three percent."

"Three percent?" both agents exploded, and this time even Irv chimed in: "You'll never see any of the AGR, anyway! What are you arguing about this for?"

"Okay, okay," I said, trying to calm the waters. "I'll back down on the AGR on one condition."

"What's that?" one of the producers asked.

"That somebody tells me what it stands for."

There was a momentary pause on the line, which I was hoping would be followed by laughter, the release of tension, but it was not. After everyone had had a few seconds to absorb the depths of my ignorance, Irv said, "Adjusted gross receipts."

I said thank you, and all the grown-ups moved on.

Another brilliant French horn solo to add to my career.

So why do I still have an agent at all? Why do any of my writer friends, like Ted or Karen, keep an agent on the payroll? Chiefly, because we have to; you need the agent, ostensibly, to find the work and close the deals.

That's not to say there isn't another way. You *can* get rid of the agent—and many top-notch writers have done so—by replacing him with a lawyer, one who knows his way around entertainment law.

Taking the lawyerly route does confer a couple of advantages.

Lawyers are better trained to read a contract and defend your interests, and they generally will cost you less in the long run; many of them work for a 5 percent commission, and others will simply charge by the clock. Their rates can be high—several hundred bucks an hour—but in most cases that will still work out to less than an agency's flat 10 percent would. Any manager can easily recommend an attorney or two, if that's the way you decide to go, but even I wouldn't recommend it—not for newcomers. Lawyers aren't out there hustling, or combing through *Daily Variety*, the way that agents are supposed to be doing. Bigshot writers don't have to worry about finding work; the work finds them. But when you're starting out, it's still a much better idea to take the traditional agency route. Save the lawyers, and maybe even the managers for that matter, for when you've got a few credits under your belt. Then, you can reconsider.

Of course, there's always the option of going it alone, of just making your way through the Hollywood jungle without any representation at all. But if you're not a law school graduate, and you've never been an agent or worked for one, you might just as well walk to the corner of Wilshire and Doheny, strip yourself naked, and paint "Take me!" on your chest in big red letters.

Because you will be taken.

Between Jobs

■■■ In Hollywood, one thing is worth remembering: You're never out of work—you're just between jobs.

In a town where illusion is the stock-in-trade, you never want to give the impression that things aren't going well. I remember one of the first writers I met out here exuberantly telling me, "I've got six screenplays selling around town right now!"

I was bowled over—*six screenplays, selling all at once*—until I got in my car and thought about it. *Six screenplays? Selling?* What did that actually mean? Unless I was mistaken, it sounded to me, upon reflection, as if the guy had written, on spec, six screenplays . . . but that so far the reason they were all still "selling" was because nobody had actually wanted to buy any of them. While I could admire his industry (six completed screenplays), his track record (no sales) wasn't exactly something to boast about.

And yet, boast he had.

While I am in no way recommending that you join the ranks of phonies, braggarts, and poseurs who clog the streets and sidewalks of L.A., nattering into their cell phones about pilots and points and back-end deals, I *am* suggesting that you soft-pedal your own slow periods and professional doldrums. Your enemies will only exult at your troubles, and your friends, while condoling, will secretly feel relief (*thank God it's not me!*) and then find, deep in their hearts, some way to blame you for the problems you're having.

You should have written another spec!

You shouldn't have switched agents!

You should have completed your course credits for a teaching degree!

Anything, just so long as they can latch on to some reason to account for your tribulations.

Because, once they've done that, they can comfort themselves by thinking, *Well, as long as I don't do* that, *I'll be okay.* It's all voodoo, of course, but in a city where the girl at the bar may be 30 percent silicone and people believe that a fern above the toilet will keep money from getting flushed from the premises, it passes for science.

What *do* you do when you are waiting for your next assignment? Certainly, you do all the things we've already talked about—you write new spec scripts, you throw some hot concepts into your Brilliant Idea File, you call your agent.

But you also network. Once you've joined the Writers Guild, you are often invited to "member outreach" events, where a dinner is served, some outstanding issue is debated, and you can mix and mingle with your peers. Not everyone in the room with you may be an Academy Award winner, but you can be sure that they are all professional writers, with real credits, on real movies, or real TV shows. You can't imagine how refreshing that is after living in L.A. for a while.

And although professional etiquette would dictate that you keep your overt hustling to a minimum, it's nice all the same to spend a little time trading news and gossip and making new acquaintances.

This is also the time when you might want to check your account at the Favor Bank; you might discover that you have built up a healthy balance, from which you could now make a withdrawal. Did you ever, for example, give a freelance assignment to someone when you were on staff at a show (as I had done for that guy at the Universal meeting)? If so, it might be worth looking up that person now, and seeing if he or she is in a position to return the favor. Did you ever volunteer to read a friend's spec script and give him notes? Maybe it's worth having that friend read your spec script now; he might even know someone who's looking for a property like that.

Did you ever meet a studio exec who asked for your input on a project? Give her a call to say hi, and see what ever came of it. Maybe she knows of some work that's now available.

Once you've made some inroads into the TV industry and racked up a few credits, you'll see for yourself one of the reasons it was so hard to get in in the first place.

TV writers take care of their own, even when they don't like each other. I'll never forget the day, back when I was struggling to get into TV at all, that I got a call from a good friend, a well-established TV producer, who wanted the number of another TV writer, named Alex, that I happened to know socially. While I looked it up in my Rolodex, I couldn't help asking him, "So why do you want to get in touch with Alex? I thought you said he was a total hack."

"He is," my friend said. "But the guy across the street from me is running a time-travel show, and he needs staff writers badly."

"If he's that desperate," I said, "why don't you give him my number?"

"Come on," my friend said, "he's a man with a family. I can't do that to him."

My friend laughed, I tried to (never show them the blood that they've drawn), and I gave him Alex's phone number.

Alex didn't get the job either. Not that that made me feel any better, but I'd caught an important glimpse of how things were done inside the clubhouse. You did a favor—or *pretended* to do a favor—for another club member so that you could call on that same member in return if you ever needed a favor yourself. My producer friend had now done a favor, of sorts, for Alex, and Alex, if he was ever called upon to reciprocate, would have to do something for the producer. You seldom, if ever, went *outside* the clubhouse, because what good would it do you to help out somebody who might never be able to give you something back? You'd have to be betting on that person's ability to stay in the business and prosper, so that he'd one day be in a position to do something for you. How much easier it was to hand out work and assignments to other writers that you already knew. For one, they were professionals who knew the ropes, but more importantly, there was a much better chance that they'd be on staff somewhere else someday, and possibly at a time when you were not . . . when you were *between jobs* and needed some help.

It's all called playing the angles.

Read the trades, especially when you're starting out. Some of my friends subscribe to the *Hollywood Reporter*, others swear by *Daily Variety*. I'm a *Variety* man myself—I think the writing is better and more fun: Disney's the "mouse house," quitting is "ankling," PR outfits are "praiseries." But whichever publication you pick up, it'll give you a quick survey of what's happening in the industry—who's where, who's buying what, which shows have been renewed, which ones have had their tickets punched.

Can I honestly say that by reading *Variety* every day I have ever found a single piece of work that I can point to and say, "That, I got because of something I read in *Variety*"?

No, I can't.

But I do know that by reading it, I get a sense of where things are going, what kinds of shows are hot, and which ones are fading. It means that when I do talk to my agent, or manager, or anyone else in the business, I know who *they're* referring to, I know what trend they're tapping into, I know what *they* think they know (from reading the trades). It gives me an aerial view of the terrain, and in some ways that does help me to target my strikes. By the way, the subscription cost—which at present is $219 a year for *Variety*—is tax deductible.

Or you can do as so many screen and TV writers do in L.A.— buy a cup of coffee in the café at the local bookstore, and read the trades right there. If you do choose this "free read" option, however, please be courteous to the TV writer who will inevitably follow you, and keep the pages free of crumbs and coffee stains.

Isn't this the least we can do for each other?

And there's always the mail. When you're between jobs, getting the mail is good for at least a couple of minutes every day, because, make no mistake, TV is the business that keeps on giving. Why, only yesterday I grumpily pried the mail out of the box only to find, lurking among the credit card bills and Domino's flyers, a telltale pale green envelope.

This, my friends, is the color of good news. It is the color of the oversized envelopes that the Writers Guild uses to mail out your residuals, which can come at virtually any time and in any denomination. It's a great feeling, knowing that somewhere in the world, at some time of night or day, on some station you may never even have heard of, your work has been shown—and you are now getting paid for it.

Sometimes these checks are for thousands of dollars; sometimes they're for less. (With the one I just got, I could buy a nice new suit—if I wore suits.) My wife and I usually make a little ritual out of it, which we learned from my friends Bill and Pam. We open the envelope slowly, covering up the digits on the check and only revealing them—and the full magnitude of the amount—a little at a time.

As you can see, Laurie and I lead a very uneventful life.

All I can say is, these residual checks have a way of arriving just when you need them the most. And for TV writers, who've been at this game for years, they can amount to a great deal of dough. I have one acquaintance in the business who moaned to me that she hadn't worked for an entire year, and when I expressed my sympathy, she quickly added, "Of course my residuals still topped six figures for the year, so it's not as if I couldn't pay the nanny." (See what I said about never letting any chinks in your armor show?)

As you work in the business, and your credits accumulate, you too will be looking for—and finding—these little green missives in your mailbox. Think of them as a sort of grant from the universe, money from your past that, by covering your immediate bills, enables you to focus fully on the bright future that lies before you.

Finally, and I'm probably the last person in the world who should be saying this, Keep your spirits up.

The guild did a health survey of its membership not long ago, and, as I recall, many of the most-prescribed medications were antidepressants. Prozac, Zoloft, Paxil—all those names that sound to me like characters from some cheesy sci-fi script. But no one was very surprised by these survey results.

Writers lead a solitary, and often scary, life, and there's really no getting around that. To get the work done—and eventually it must be done—you have to close the door, sit down, draw the blinds so there isn't any glare on the computer screen, and stay there, all by yourself.

Meanwhile, you'll feel like everybody else in the world is outside in the sunshine running around, laughing, talking, tossing Frisbees to the dog, flirting at Starbucks, *having a life*.

And some of them, damn it, are.

The rest of us have a job to do, and your job, unfortunately, calls for a lot of self-discipline and solitude. The rewards, however, make it all worthwhile, and that's something you must never allow yourself to forget. Unlike most folks, you are paid to dream. To tell stories. To make stuff up. To think about whatever you want to, and see where your thoughts take you . . . wherever that might be.

And your efforts *yield* something. Frankly, I've never understood how people can stand to do jobs everyday where they can never, ever point to anything and say, *I created that. That wouldn't exist without me. I thought of it, I made it happen. My name is on it.* I think it would be very hard to labor in such anonymity, to work for no other purpose than the greater good of some company. And I think, to be honest, that I'm too full of myself to do it.

Writers, I think, have to be. If you don't have, somewhere inside you, that undeniable urge to make your mark, to have your say, to create something from scratch, even if it's only a TV episode, then let me offer you this one final piece of advice before I shut up and go away. Spare yourself all the trials of the writing life—'cause sometimes, trust me, it'll seem like nothing *but* trials—and find yourself a less stressful line of work.

Like fighter pilot.

About the Author

 **Before** embarking on his career in TV, Robert Masello was an award-winning journalist and author.

His articles, essays, and reviews have appeared in such diverse publications as the *Washington Post*, *New York* magazine, *Newsday*, *Redbook*, *Elle*, *Town and Country*, *TV Guide*, *Cosmopolitan*, *Travel & Leisure*, *People* magazine, and *Harper's Bazaar*.

He has written twelve previous books, including *Fallen Angels*, *Raising Hell*, and the novel *Black Horizon*, which is currently in development for series TV. His work has been translated into eight languages.

In addition to various specials and talk-shows, his dramatic series credits include such shows as *Sliders*, *Early Edition*, and *Poltergeist: The Legacy*.

He has taught and lectured on writing at New York University, Brooklyn College, Pace University, UCLA Extension, and the Columbia University School of Journalism, where he served as an adjunct professor for five years.

A native of Evanston, Illinois, and honors graduate of Princeton University, he now lives in Santa Monica, California, with his wife, Laurie, and his trusty dog, Sam.